HOMER
ILIAD VI

Edited with Introduction,
Notes & Vocabulary by

R.H. Jordan & J.A. Harrison

Bristol Classical Press

Cover illustration: The meeting of Hektor and Andromache; detail
from an engraving of Flaxman's drawing, from *The Iliad of Homer
Engraved from the Compositions of John Flaxman*, Longman, 1805

First published in 1985 by
Bristol Classical Press
an imprint of
Gerald Duckworth & Co. Ltd
The Old Piano Factory
48 Hoxton Square, London N1 6PB

Reprinted 1990, 1995

A catalogue record for this book is available
from the British Library

ISBN 0-86292-149-X

Available in USA and Canada from:
Focus Information Group
PO Box 369
Newburyport
MA 01950

Printed in Great Britain by
Booksprint, Bristol

CONTENTS

LIST OF ILLUSTRATIONS

FOREWORD

This edition of *Iliad* VI is designed as a companion to
our previous one of *Iliad* I, and is written particularly
for those who are beginning to read Homer. This Book,
notable for its sensitive portrayal of a family caught
up in the horror of war, is an ideal study for GCSE or
at A-level.

As with the other volume, the Introduction deals briefly
with various topics related to the epic poem as a whole
and a select Bibliography is also provided. There is a
full Vocabulary, and the Notes are designed to help and
guide the reader in the translation of the Greek. In
this connection Appendix I lists commonly recurring
Homeric forms with examples taken where possible from
Book VI; this would be a helpful aid in the reading of
further books of the *Iliad*.

The other Appendices deal with Homer's use of prepositions,
formulae and metre. As the *Iliad* is oral poetry, it is
hoped that teachers will read the Greek aloud and encourage their pupils to do the same. To ignore the sound of
the poetry is to lose much of its impact.

The text used in the preparation of this volume is sub-
stantially that to be found in Professor Willcock's excellent edition of *Iliad* I-XII; help was also derived from
Munro's *Iliad*. Our sincere thanks are due to the Bristol
Classical Press whose reader and General Editor gave us
much valuable help. Lay-out is by Frances Bond and
illustrations by Jean Bees and Elizabeth Induni.

R.H. Jordan
J.A. Harrison

July 1985

Hektor departing from Andromache, with Helen and Paris on the left; Chalcidian wine-bowl (*krater*) by the Inscription Painter, ca. 540 B.C.; Martin von Wagner Museum, Würzburg.

INTRODUCTION

Homer and his importance to the Greeks

Homer occupied a unique position in the minds of the
ancient Greeks. He was regarded as an authority on
their earliest history and on relations between gods
and men. Often it was enough to quote a line from Homer's
poems or to refer to some incident in the poems to settle
a dispute. Every educated Greek in the classical period
got to know his Homer from a very early age. Homer's
stories of heroes, gods and deeds of bravery were told
to children by nurses and parents. Later on, when boys
went to school at the age of seven, the *grammatistes*,
who taught writing, reading and poetry, made his pupils
learn and recite large sections of Homer's poems from
memory.

Homer frequently provided inspiration for Greek painters
and playwrights. Vase painting, particularly at Athens,
illustrated incidents from the poems - the embassy to
Achilles (p.36), the blinding of Polyphemus (p.41) - or
from the Trojan cycle - the sack of Troy (p.64). The
writers of tragedy went back time and again to the great
heroic figures of Homer's poetry for their subjects. The
Agamemnon of Aeschylus, Sophocles' *Ajax* and *Philoctetes*
and many of Euripides' plays are based on the epic cycle.
Indeed Aeschylus is supposed to have said that his plays
were merely 'slices from Homer's banquet'.

The Greeks of the classical period had opportunities of
hearing Homer recited. In the great pan-Hellenic gather-
ings such as that at Olympia and at the more local festivals
like the Panathenaea at Athens recitals from Homer were given
by professional rhapsodes (see p.76). The recitations at
Athens were possibly instituted by the tyrant Pisistratus
in the second half of the sixth century.

In spite of being so important to the Greeks and having two
masterpieces to his credit, Homer himself is a mysterious
figure. Ancient authorities had different ideas about when
he lived. Eratosthenes placed him in the twelfth century
B.C. whereas Herodotus said that he lived some five hundred
years later. Many cities claimed to be his birthplace, of
which Smyrna and Chios were the most notable. A family on
Chios had the name Homeridae - descendants of Homer - and,
as professional rhapsodes, helped to maintain the tradition
of Homeric poetry. Other epics and poems were attributed
to Homer in ancient times, e.g. the *Thebais*, an epic poem
about the city of Thebes, and the so-called *Homeric Hymns*;
but the real authors of these are unknown. There was a
legend that Homer was blind and some have claimed that the

1

blind bard Demodocus who appears in Book VIII of the
Odyssey is a self-portrait of Homer.

So Homer is very much a mystery. All that is really
known of him is that two of the greatest epic poems ever
created are firmly attached to his name. Most of the
ancient Greeks did not doubt that he was the author of
the *Iliad* and the *Odyssey* and that he was, as Plato says,
'the best and most divine of poets'. In more recent times
some scholars have held the view that the two poems were
not composed by the same person. As to when the poems
were established in the form that we have them now, most
scholars favour a date around 750 to 700 B.C. - not very
far from the date suggested by Herodotus.

Oral epic poetry

A great controversy has long raged about the way in which
the Homeric poems were composed. Were they the work of
one man? Were the poems put together from other compositions now lost? Recent research into epic poetry, and
especially the oral epic poetry of Jugoslavia, has given
us a new insight into some of those questions. Oral epic
of the heroic kind is also found in the Icelandic sagas,
the French *Chanson de Roland* and the Irish heroic cycles.

Even in the ancient world it was realised that the language
of Homer was highly artificial. It is made up of forms and
words drawn from different Greek dialects and incorporated
at different times. No Greek ever spoke in the dialect of
Homer. With the knowledge we now have of oral epic poetry
we can be sure that the *Iliad* and the *Odyssey* are the products of a long tradition of such poetry.

Anyone who reads Homer even in translation soon notices
that certain phrases, and even whole lines, occur more than
once. These stock phrases are known as 'formulae' (see
Appendix 3 below). The poet had a wide selection of them
at his disposal and became skilled at selecting suitable
ones and fitting them into the story he was telling.

Obviously to become a poet of this kind required many
years of training. During this training the young bard
would listen to masters of the craft and add to his repertoire
of stories. Each telling of these great stories - or rather
the chanting of them to the accompaniment of the lyre - was
to some extent a new creation with room for individual styles.
Certainly no two performances would have been exactly the same
word for word. A skilled bard could easily tailor his story
to his audience by inserting an apposite simile or by refer-

ring to heroes and incidents in their city's past.

Usually a bard would give a rendering of one episode from a collection dealing with the Trojan War or the Return of the Heroes. A performance of anything like the full *Iliad* or *Odyssey* must have been over a number of sessions, if at all. These poems in the form that we have them are more like special compositions drawing together a large number of related episodes. They may be the work of a master poet working at a time when the tradition of oral poetry was beginning to wane. It seems probable that Homer was that master poet but this can never be certain.

The Mycenaean Age and Homer

Archaeology has given us some ideas of the way of life which characterised the real Mycenaean age. Mycenae, the legendary city of Agamemnon, has been excavated and shown to have been the centre of power in that area. The massive stone walls of the fortress and the beautifully built beehive tombs which still remain prove that Mycenae had a succession of powerful rulers. Remains of other important centres have been found at Tiryns (close to Mycenae), at Pylos in the S.W. Peloponnese, at Thebes in Boeotia and at Volos in Thessaly.

Many people know of the gold masks and crowns which were found in the grave circles at Mycenae, but many other objects have been unearthed - painted pottery, rings, brooches, ivory carvings, frescoes, weapons and religious vessels (see p.39). All these objects help to give us an idea of the kind of society that existed in the centres of Mycenaean power. As is often the case, it is the lifestyle of the nobility and the most powerful that we know most about.

However, thanks to a fire at Pylos we now have a detailed record of the administration of a Mycenaean kingdom. During the burning of the palace, baskets of clay tablets were baked hard and the writing on them was preserved. On these tablets are the notes made by clerks in the palace recording various items of produce, lists of animals and groups of people. The impression these records give us is that the palace and its administration had a very precise control over the people and products of the kingdom. In many ways this information complements the more spectacular finds from Mycenae and elsewhere.

Greece in the Mycenaean age was not a unified country but was split up into certain areas, probably kingdoms. Each was separately governed and highly organised by a central authority. Trading was carried on with Crete (where clay

tablets, similar to those from Pylos, have also been found
at Knossos (see p.28)), Egypt and other areas in the eastern Mediterranean. Life for the Mycenaean Greeks - for
the ruling classes at least - was rich and interesting.

When we look at the Mycenaean age as portrayed by Homer,
we find an idealised and one-sided view. Since the poems
were composed and retold to glorify the ruling families,
this one-sided view is only to be expected. Little men-
tion is made of the ordinary people in the poems - a mere
handful of them have names. We are only dimly aware of them
serving in the ranks of the armies, labouring away in the
background on their tenant farms, or in their small work-
shops. The centre of the stage is held exclusively by the
heroes: Odysseus, Achilles, Hektor, Agamemnon, Ajax and
others. There is a greater gulf between the nobles and
peasants than between nobles and gods.

The nobles in the poems live in splendour. Homer describes
elaborate palaces where feasting seems to be the order of
every day. Since the poetry was recalling a bygone age, such
exaggerated descriptions were not likely to have been doubt-
ed and besides they contributed to the prestige of the heroes.
The life of the heroes is devoted to the gaining of glory.
This means fighting in wars where bravery and skill at arms
can be demonstrated and where loot such as gold, silver,
slaves and cattle can be won. The noble families also prove
their superiority by giving and receiving presents: the
value or status of the present adds to the prestige of the
giver and receiver. What Agamemnon says about the prize
Chryseis in Book I 118-119 and 135-136 provides an instance.

Inferior to the nobles are groups ranging from free tenant
farmers, people with specially prized skills (blacksmiths,
priests, doctors, bards, workers in precious metals) down to
bought slaves. These people work for the nobles and those
who are not slaves always run the risk of losing their freedom as a result of raiding or a full scale war. In the poems
they make little contribution to the action. In the *Iliad*
they sit patiently through the assembly in the camp, never
being asked to speak, or they flee in battle from great
warriors like Hektor.

Homer preserves in broad outline a Mycenaean setting: the
kingdoms with separate kings, bronze as the usual metal,
boars-tusk helmets (see p.12) and the huge body shield
which Ajax carries. But other later practices have been incorporated in the poetic tradition. The heroes are described
as cremating fallen warriors whereas archaeology tells us
that the Mycenaeans buried their dead. Although the
geography of the Mycenaean world has been preserved fairly
accurately, for example in the catalogue of troops in Book

II, the Phoenicians - those intrepid merchants of a later period - make a brief appearance in the *Iliad*.

Whether or not we think that epic poetry began during the Mycenaean period itself, it was in the later periods that epic poems like the *Iliad* and *Odyssey* flourished. The historic Mycenaean period ended in the fall of the kingdoms and with them was swept away much of the fabric of civilised life. In the succeeding periods - the so-called Dark Age and the early Geometric Period - danger and uncertainty prevailed to such an extent that large numbers of people gradually left their homes, particularly in areas like the Argolid, eastern Attica, Laconia and Boeotia and fled in most cases eastwards across the Aegean. In their new homes they kept alive in poetic tradition memories of their past, though, as new techniques and social developments came about, their heroic past became more and more remote and idealised. These periods were ones when burial practices changed, first to cremation and later back to inhumation. The Homeric heroes were always cremated and so follow not the Mycenaean but the Dark Age custom in this important respect. The ritual connected with burial as described in the *Iliad* seems to be close to that portrayed on some Geometric pottery (see p.53). The centralised bureaucratic kingdoms with their elaborate organisation that we glimpse in the Mycenaean tablets has vanished, but it is safe to assume that at least for a time petty kings ruled in various parts of the Greek world with a band of nobles not far below them in rank. The feuding state of Odysseus' kingdom, described for us in the *Odyssey*, must belong to the Dark Age. These kings and nobles, who possibly claimed descent from Ajax and Agamemnon, provided the epic story-tellers with audiences and perhaps with patronage. By the time that the epic poems were written down, the Greeks had emerged from the Dark Age and the Geometric Period was well established everywhere. Kingship had given way to aristocracy, the eastern Mediterranean was regularly crossed and recrossed by Greek and Phoenician traders, a totally new system of writing, based on the Phoenician alphabet, had been introduced and Greek communities were looking forward to a new and prosperous era.

We know from archaeology that a city on the site where Troy was thought to have stood was destroyed by fire at about the right time, but this does not prove that the Greeks went to Troy and burned it, or that a man named Agamemnon ruled at Mycenae. Also we would be misguided if we were to suppose that Homer's poems set out to provide a factual and accurate account of historical events. That there is a kernel of historical truth in the poems - especially in the *Iliad* - is seldom disputed. The dispute is about the size of that kernel. Homer aims to praise nobility of action and greatness of character. Exaggerated descriptions of king's

palaces and inflated casualty lists help to create this
heroic image: literal historical truth is not the prime
consideration.

The Iliad

The name 'Iliad' comes from 'Ilion', one of the names of
Troy. The Greek siege of Troy traditionally lasted ten
years so it might seem that the twenty-four books of the
poem match in length the scale of the war. But in fact
the events described in the poem cover only a few days
during the tenth year of the siege.

The title 'Iliad' is, in fact, a misnomer. The poem's
theme is 'The Anger of Achilles', its cause, its results
and the final appeasement of that anger. A brief summary
of the story will make this clear.

The 'Anger' started when Agamemnon, leader of the Greek
forces, is compelled to give up his own war-prize Chryseis
and takes away Briseis, Achilles' prize (see p.18).
Achilles is dissuaded by Athene from killing Agamemnon but
withdraws his forces from the war and sits gloomy and sulking
in his hut in the Greek camp. The Greeks, deprived of their
best warrior, suffer serious reverses during which the Trojans, led by Hektor, start to burn the Greek ships.
Agamemnon sends a peace mission to Achilles with lavish
gifts but the hero is unmoved. Then Patroklos, Achilles'
closest friend (see p.14), worried about the safety of the
Greek army, persuades Achilles to lend him his armour.
The Trojans, believing Achilles has again taken the field,
are driven back until Hektor recognises Patroklos and kills
him in single combat. Achilles, crazed with grief, sets
aside his quarrel and renews the fight. He eventually
meets and   slays Hektor whose body he ties to his chariot
and drags round the walls of Troy. Funeral games are held
in honour of Patroklos (see p.37). Priam, king of Troy
and father of Hektor, comes to Achilles' hut to beg for the
body of his son and even kisses the hands that had slain so
many of his children. Achilles at last is moved to pity and
surrenders the body for burial. The 'Anger' is appeased and
the poem ends with the mourning Trojans at the funeral of
Hektor.

A large part of the poem is taken up with war scenes and
contests between warriors (pp.24, 34 & 43). Homer uses
many devices - strange modes of attack, unexpected outcomes,
recognition scenes etc. - to avoid monotony. The climate
in which the leading warriors live is very much one of
'death or glory'. A victory over a worthy opponent raises
the victor in the ranks of the heroes. There is no sporting
aspect to these contests. You taunt your opponent before

the fight and insult him in defeat.

But the poem is not just one combat after another. We are
given clear pictures of the main characters - the arrogant
Agamemnon, hot-headed Achilles, cunning Odysseus (p.36),
stolid Ajax, long-winded Nestor (p.51). We look inside the
beleaguered city and see Helen sitting on the wall with the
Trojan elders and pointing out the various Greek heroes in
the plain beneath. In this book we hear Hektor scold his
foppish brother Paris and later say goodbye to Andromache
his wife and his little son (p.59) as he goes out to the
battle from which he never returns.

Presiding over this complex web of action are the gods,
looking down from their home on Mount Olympus. The gods
resemble the human heroes except that they are stronger
and are not subject to death. They take sides in the war.
Hera and Athene are pro-Greek; Ares and Aphrodite pro-
Trojan. Apollo is variable but more often on the Trojan
side. Poor Zeus does his best to remain neutral amid the
complaints and entreaties of the other gods! The gods
descend from Olympus to join in the fighting or to pro-
tect their favourites, often by supernatural means but in
human disguises. The picture of the family on Olympus
is a very human one. Its members laugh and cry, quarrel
and make love, gossip and scheme like children on earth.
Father Zeus and his wife Hera often fall out as Zeus
asserts his masculine authority and Hera gets round him
with her womanly wiles (see p.81).

The *Iliad* is not just a war poem. It does describe hero-
ism and cowardice on the field of battle but, more than
that, it shows us a recognisable group of human beings and
how they react to each other and to the war.

Book Six of the *Iliad*

The two great champions in the *Iliad* are Achilles the Greek
and Hektor the Trojan. Book I shows us the proud hot-headed
Achilles whose anger is the theme of the whole epic. In
Books I to V we see Hektor as a war leader but learn little
of him as a man. It is Book VI which does for Hektor what
Book I does for Achilles.

The two leaders are alike in some things: their prowess in
battle, their adherence to the heroic code and their fatal-
istic attitude to death; but whereas Achilles is a ruthless
fighting-machine, Hektor is a husband and a father as well
as a warrior. The scene on the walls of Troy with Hektor and
Andromache and their son Astyanax is rightly regarded as one
of the highlights of the whole poem. The more human side of

Hektor is seen in his love for his wife and son and his
sorrow at what must befall them after the capture of Troy.
For Hektor is a fatalist. He knows that Troy will fall and
what will happen to the Trojan women and children there-
after. He does his best to comfort his wife but it is cold
comfort. He brushes aside her pleas that he stay within
the walls and defend the city from there. His place is in
the forefront of the battle and he will not meet his death
there till it is so fated - for no one can escape from fate.
As he returns to the fray, he kisses his son and bids
Andromache return to their home. She goes off with many a
backward look and many a sad tear.

At the beginning of Book VI we see how Homer avoids monotony in recounting numerous killings. There are many simple
statements that A killed B and C killed D. But there are
also odd details to fill out the picture and add variety
and interest. Diomedes' victim Axulos had many friends
but none was there when he needed them. Euryalos kills the
twin sons of a nymph. Adrestos gets entangled in his chariot
reins and would have been ransomed by Menelaus had not
Agamemnon arrived and killed him. Diomedes and Glaukos do
not fight at all. They discover they are family guest-
friends, exchange armour and decide to avoid one another
in the battle.

As Diomedes is routing the Trojans, Hektor is persuaded to
return to the city. He urges his mother to organise prayers
to Athene, refuses the hospitality of Helen and upbraids
Paris for skulking at home. After Hektor has met his wife
and son, he and Paris return to the battle.

So-called 'Cup of Nestor' from Shaft Grave
IV at Mycenae; National Museum, Athens.

SELECT BIBLIOGRAPHY

This bibliography is divided into two sections: A is regarded as suitable for readers preparing for Ordinary
Level GCE examinations and GCSEs at 15+; and B for older
students coming to Homer for the first time.

SECTION A

Thorpe, M.

Homer (Macmillan, 1973 - Inside the Ancient World Series).

Baldry, H.C.

Ancient Greek Literature in its Living Context, ch. 1 (Thames & Hudson, 1968).

Bolton, J.

Ancient Crete and Mycenae (Longman, 1968 - Then and There Series).

Andrewes, A.

Greek Society, ch. 2 & 3 (Pelican, 1971).

Bowra, C.M.

Landmarks in Greek Literature (Pelican, 1965).

Finley, M.I.

The World of Odysseus (Chatto & Windus, 1956; Pelican, 1962).

Chadwick, J.

The Mycenaean World (Cambridge University Press, 1976).

Griffin, J.

Homer (Oxford University Press, 1980 - Past Masters Series).

SECTION B

Kirk, G.S.

Homer and the Epic (Cambridge University Press, 1976).

Kirk, G.S.

Homer and the Oral Tradition (Cambridge University Press, 1976).

Camps, W.A.

An Introduction to Homer (Oxford University Press, 1980).

Trypanis, C.A.

The Homeric Epics (Aris & Phillips, 1977).

Mireaux, E.

Everyday Life in the Time of Homer (George Allen & Unwin, 1959).

Finnegan, R. (ed.)	*The Penguin Book of Oral Poetry* (Penguin, 1978).
Finley, M.I.	*Early Greece: the Bronze and Archaic Ages* (Chatto & Windus, 1970).
Webster, T.B.L.	*From Mycenae to Homer* (Methuen, 1977 - 2nd ed.).
Wace, A.J.B. & Stubbings, F.H.	*A Companion to Homer* (Macmillan, 1962).
Bowra, C.M.	*Homer* (Duckworth, 1972).
Griffin, J.	*Homer on Life and Death* (Oxford University Press, 1980).
Mueller, M.	*The Iliad* (George Allen & Unwin, 1984).

Paris abducting Helen, assisted by Aeneas, Eros, Aphrodite and Peitho (Persuasion). From an early fifth century B.C. cup (*skyphos*) of the Attic red-figure style by the painter Makron (whose 'signature' appears behind the figure of Peitho on the extreme right); Museum of Fine Arts, Boston.

ΙΛΙΑΔΟΣ Ζ

Ἕκτορος καὶ Ἀνδρομάχης ὁμιλία

Τρώων δ' οἰώθη καὶ Ἀχαιῶν φύλοπις αἰνή·
πολλὰ δ' ἄρ' ἔνθα καὶ ἔνθ' ἴθυσε μάχη πεδίοιο
ἀλλήλων ἰθυνομένων χαλκήρεα δοῦρα,
μεσσηγὺς Σιμόεντος ἰδὲ Ξάνθοιο ῥοάων.

Ajax and other Achaian chiefs slay various Trojans.

Αἴας δὲ πρῶτος Τελαμώνιος, ἕρκος Ἀχαιῶν,   5
Τρώων ῥῆξε φάλαγγα, φόως δ' ἑτάροισιν ἔθηκεν,
ἄνδρα βαλών, ὃς ἄριστος ἐνὶ Θρήκεσσι τέτυκτο,
υἱὸν Ἐυσσώρου Ἀκάμαντ' ἠύν τε μέγαν τε.
τόν ῥ' ἔβαλε πρῶτος κόρυθος φάλον ἱπποδασείης,
ἐν δὲ μετώπῳ πῆξε, πέρησε δ' ἄρ' ὀστέον εἴσω   10
αἰχμὴ χαλκείη· τὸν δὲ σκότος ὄσσε κάλυψεν.
Ἄξυλον δ' ἄρ' ἔπεφνε βοὴν ἀγαθὸς Διομήδης

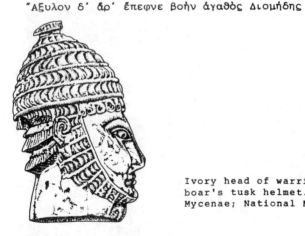

Ivory head of warrior wearing
boar's tusk helmet. From
Mycenae; National Museum, Athens.

NOTES

(HF *refers to Homeric Forms (see Appendix 1): only a few
examples of each form are referred to in the notes.*)

1   At the end of Book V the gods return to Olympos and we
    are left to see what the heroes can do without divine
    help.
    οἰώθη: 'was left alone' (i.e. by the gods).

2   πολλά: adv. 'far and wide'.
    πεδίοιο: 'over the plain', taken with ἔνθα καὶ ἔνθα.
    For -οιο ending, HF 5A.

3   ἀλλήλων ἰθυνομένων: with μάχη, 'of them as they aimed
    at each other'.
    χαλκήρεα: endings often left uncontracted in the epic
    dialect, HF 6B.
    δοῦρα: HF 1B.

4   The two rivers flowing over the Trojan plain.
    Ξάνθοιο: HF 5A.
    ῥοάων: HF 4C.

5   πρῶτος: Ajax is the first of three Greek heroes whose
    exploits in battle are highlighted. The other two,
    Diomedes and Euryalos, appear at 12 and 20 respect-
    ively.
    Τελαμώνιος: a patronymic. Telamon was king in Salamis.

6   ῥῆξε for ἔρρηξε: HF 10A.
    ἑτάροισιν: HF 5B.
    ἔθηκεν: 'brought'.

7   Θρήκεσσι: HF 6A.
    τέτυκτο: 'was'.

8   The description of Akamas, including the reference to
    his father, is to enhance the feat of Ajax.

9   τόν: HF 20A.
    ἔβαλε: governing two accusatives: one (τόν) the person
    as a whole, and the other (φάλον) the particular part
    concerned. See 11 for another example.
    κόρυθος φάλον: a much disputed phrase. It is thought
    that φάλος means either a horn-like projection on the
    helmet or the slot into which the plume was fitted.

10 εἴσω: adv. 'within'.

11 αἰχμή: subject of πῆξε and πέρησε: see also HF 10A

12 βοὴν ἀγαθός: 'good at the war-cry'. βοήν is accus. of
    respect defining the force of the adjective.

Τευθρανίδην, ὃς ἔναιεν ἐϋκτιμένῃ ἐν Ἀρίσβῃ
ἀφνειὸς βιότοιο, φίλος δ' ἦν ἀνθρώποισιν·
πάντας γὰρ φιλέεσκεν ὁδῷ ἔπι οἰκία ναίων.   15
ἀλλά οἱ οὔ τις τῶν γε τότ' ἤρκεσε λυγρὸν ὄλεθρον
πρόσθεν ὑπαντιάσας, ἀλλ' ἄμφω θυμὸν ἀπηύρα,
αὐτὸν καὶ θεράποντα Καλήσιον, ὅς ῥα τόθ' ἵππων
ἔσκεν ὑφηνίοχος· τὼ δ' ἄμφω γαῖαν ἐδύτην.

Δρῆσον δ' Εὐρύαλος καὶ Ὀφέλτιον ἐξενάριξεν·   20
βῆ δὲ μετ' Αἴσηπον καὶ Πήδασον, οὕς ποτε νύμφη
νηὶς Ἀβαρβαρέη τέκ' ἀμύμονι Βουκολίωνι.
Βουκολίων δ' ἦν υἱὸς ἀγαυοῦ Λαομέδοντος
πρεσβύτατος γενεῇ, σκότιον δέ ἑ γείνατο μήτηρ·
ποιμαίνων δ' ἐπ' ὄεσσι μίγη φιλότητι καὶ εὐνῇ,   25
ἡ δ' ὑποκυσαμένη διδυμάονε γείνατο παῖδε.

Achilles binds the wounds of Patroclus; from interior of wine-
cup (*kylix*) by the Sosias Painter, ca. 500 B.C.; Berlin.

13   Axylos was a worthy opponent for Diomedes, not perhaps for his prowess in war but he was a wealthy man and most hospitable. Sadly not one of his friends was at hand to help him (see 16-19).

14   βιότοιο: HF 5A, descriptive genitive, 'rich in ...'.
ἀνθρώποισιν: HF 5B. φίλος ... ἀνθρώποισιν probably means 'he was a popular person'.

15   φιλέεσκεν: HF 13, 'he used to entertain'.
ἐπι: with ὁδῷ. Note the change of accent on ἐπί when it stands after its noun (see Appendix 2B).
οἰκία ναίων: ναίω is often followed by a direct object (see also 34-5), 'living in a house on the (main) road'.

16   οἱ: HF 9A, 'from him'.
τῶν: HF 20A, 'of them', i.e. his guests.

17   πρόσθεν ὑπαντιάσας: 'going to meet (Diomedes) in front of him (Axylos)'.
ἄμφω θυμόν: two accusatives after ἀπηύρα. Verbs of robbing or depriving often take two accusatives. See 70-71.

18   αὐτόν: '(the great man) himself'.

19   ἔσκεν: HF 13.
τὼ δ' ἄμφω γαῖαν ἐδύτην: dual endings, 'and both of them went below the earth'.

20   Euryalos is one of the leaders of the contingent from the Argolid.

21ff. The poet brings variety and interest to his description of killing by elaborating on the family history of the victims.

21-22 βῆ and τέκ(ε): HF 10A.
μετ(ά): 'in pursuit of'.

23-24 It looks as if Boukolion was an illegitimate elder brother of Priam.

24   γενεῇ: HF 1A.
ἑ: HF 9A.

25   ἐπ(ί): 'in charge of'.
ὄεσσι: HF 6A.
The phrase μίγη φιλότητι καὶ εὐνῇ is the formula for 'had sexual intercourse'.

26   ἥ: Ἀβαρβερέη.
διδυμάονε ... παῖδε: dual accusatives, 'twin boys'.

καὶ μὲν τῶν ὑπέλυσε μένος καὶ φαίδιμα γυῖα

Μηκιστηιάδης καὶ ἀπ' ὤμων τεύχε· ἐσύλα.

'Αστύαλον δ' ἄρ' ἔπεφνε μενεπτόλεμος Πολυποίτης·

Πιδύτην δ' 'Οδυσεὺς Περκώσιον ἐξενάριξεν   30

ἔγχεϊ χαλκείῳ, Τεῦκρος δ' 'Αρετάονα δῖον.

'Αντίλοχος δ' "Αβληρον ἐνήρατο δουρὶ φαεινῷ

Νεστορίδης, "Ελατον δὲ ἄναξ ἀνδρῶν 'Αγαμέμνων·

ναῖε δὲ Σατνιόεντος ἐϋρρείταο παρ' ὄχθας

Πήδασον αἰπεινήν. Φύλακον δ' ἕλε Λήιτος ἥρως   35

φεύγοντ'· Εὐρύπυλος δὲ Μελάνθιον ἐξενάριξεν.

Agamemnon persuades Menelaos not to take Adrestos alive.

"Αδρηστον δ' ἄρ' ἔπειτα βοὴν ἀγαθὸς Μενέλαος

ζωὸν ἕλ'· ἵππω γάρ οἱ ἀτυζομένω πεδίοιο

ὄζῳ ἔνι βλαφθέντε μυρικίνῳ, ἀγκύλον ἅρμα

ἄξαντ' ἐν πρώτῳ ῥυμῷ αὐτὼ μὲν ἐβήτην   40

πρὸς πόλιν, ᾗ περ οἱ ἄλλοι ἀτυζόμενοι φοβέοντο,

αὐτὸς δ' ἐκ δίφροιο παρὰ τροχὸν ἐξεκυλίσθη

πρηνὴς ἐν κονίῃσιν ἐπὶ στόμα. πὰρ δέ οἱ ἔστη

Late Mycenaean soldier carrying
single spear and wearing small,
roughly circular body-shield.
From the 'Warrior Vase' dis-
covered at Mycenae; National
Museum, Athens.

27   τῶν: HF 20B.

28   Μηκιστηιάδης: a patronymic. Patronymic endings in
        -ίδης or -άδης are a common feature of epic dialect.
        τεύχε(α): HF 6B. It was usual to strip armour from a
        slain enemy. Besides its value, it brought extra
        glory to its new owner.

29-36   In these lines the poet mentions other warriors briefly
        to illustrate his picture of widespread warfare across
        the Trojan plain (see 2).

29   Polypoetes was leader of the Lapiths.

33   Nestor himself is present in the Greek army, see 66.

34   ἐυρρείταο: HF 4B.

35   Leitos was one of the leaders of the Boeotian con-
        tingent.

36   Eurypylos was leader of a band of Thessalians.

37   Ἄδρηστον: not to be confused with Adrastos the leg-
        endary king of Argos.
        βοὴν ἀγαθός: this phrase has already been applied to
        Diomedes (12).

38   ἐλ': i.e. ἔλε (aor. of αἱρέω).
        ἵππω: nominative dual; five further duals in agree-
        ment follow.
        οἱ: HF 9A, 'his'.
        πεδίοιο: see 2.

39   βλαφθέντε: dual, 'becoming entangled'.
        ἔνι: with ὄζῳ, see note on ἔπι, 15.

40   ἐν πρώτῳ ῥυμῷ: 'at the top of the pole'.
        αὐτώ: 'the horses (ἵππω, 38) (by) themselves'.

41   ᾗ περ: 'to the very place where'.
        ἀτυζόμενοι φοβέοντο: 'were rushing in fear'. See also
        HF 18B.

42   αὐτός: often refers to the master or owner, see 18.

43   κονίῃσιν: HF 4D.
        πὰρ ... ἔστη: tmesis for παρέστη, aorist of παρίσταμαι,
        see Appendix 2C; for πὰρ see HF 2C.

'Ατρείδης Μενέλαος ἔχων δολιχόσκιον ἔγχος·

"Αδρηστος δ' ἄρ' ἔπειτα λαβὼν ἐλλίσσετο γούνων   45

"ζώγρει, 'Ατρέος υἱέ, σὺ δ' ἄξια δέξαι ἄποινα.

πολλὰ δ' ἐν ἀφνειοῦ πατρὸς κειμήλια κεῖται,

χαλκός τε χρυσός τε πολύκμητός τε σίδηρος·

τῶν κέν τοι χαρίσαιτο πατὴρ ἀπερείσι' ἄποινα,

εἴ κεν ἐμὲ ζωὸν πεπύθοιτ' ἐπὶ νηυσὶν 'Αχαιῶν."   50

ὣς φάτο, τῷ δ' ἄρα θυμὸν ἐνὶ στήθεσσιν ἔπειθεν.

καὶ δή μιν τάχ' ἔμελλε θοὰς ἐπὶ νῆας 'Αχαιῶν

δώσειν ᾧ θεράποντι καταξέμεν· ἀλλ' 'Αγαμέμνων

ἀντίος ἦλθε θέων, καὶ ὁμοκλήσας ἔπος ηὔδα·

"ὦ πέπον, ὦ Μενέλαε, τί ἦ δὲ σὺ κήδεαι οὕτως   55

ἀνδρῶν; ἦ σοὶ ἄριστα πεποίηται κατὰ οἶκον

πρὸς Τρώων; τῶν μή τις ὑπεκφύγοι αἰπὺν ὄλεθρον

Menelaus retrieving his wife Helen before the seated
figure of Priam; to the left stands Chryses and his
daughter Chryseis.

44 After the bustle of the last few lines there is a sudden
chilling halt. Adrastos comes to rest battered and
bruised and there standing over him is Menelaos with
his spear.

45 ἑλλίσσετο: HF 2A.
γούνων: with λαβών. Clasping a person's knees is a
sign of supplication in the Homeric poems.

46 ζώγρει: 2nd sing. imperative.

47 ἐν ἀφνειοῦ πατρός: supply δόμῳ with ἐν.

48 σίδηρος: Homer describes a society using bronze for
its day to day needs. Iron is only mentioned
occasionally.

49 τῶν: HF 20C.
τοι: as often for σοι, HF 9A.

50 πεπύθοιτ(ο): 'if he were to find out that I ...'.

51 ὣς φάτο: one of a number of standard formulae here
indicating to the listener that Adrastos' speech
is finished and the poet is resuming the story.
τῷ: HF 20A, 'his' with θυμόν.
στήθεσσι: HF 6A.
ἔπειθεν: 'he was beginning to persuade'. Compare aor.
at 61, 'he fully persuaded' or 'he convinced'.

52 μιν: 'him', HF 9A.
καὶ δή μιν τάχ' ἔμελλε: emphatic opening, 'and indeed
he was just on the point of ...'. This with the
following lines brings out a contrast in the characters of Menelaos and Agamemnon, the one soft-
hearted, the other ruthless.

53 ᾧ: from ὅς, ἥ, ὄν, 'his', HF 9B.
καταξέμεν: aor. inf. act. of κατάγω, HF 17.

54 θέων: participle of θέω, 'I run'.

55 κήδεαι: HF 11B.

56 ἦ: introducing a sarcastic enquiry.
κατὰ οἶκον: a reference to the wrong done by Paris to
Menelaos at home in Sparta.

57 τῶν: HF 20C.

57-60 The optatives ὑπεκφύγοι, φύγοι, ἐξαπολοίατο are wishes.
φέροι is either indefinite or the result of attraction.

χεῖράς θ' ἡμετέρας, μηδ' ὅν τινα γαστέρι μήτηρ

κοῦρον ἐόντα φέροι, μηδ' ὅς φύγοι, ἀλλ' ἅμα πάντες

'Ιλίου ἐξαπολοίατ' ἀκήδεστοι καὶ ἄφαντοι."   60

ὣς εἰπὼν παρέπεισεν ἀδελφεὸο φρένας ἥρως,

αἴσιμα παρειπών· ὁ δ' ἀπὸ ἔθεν ὤσατο χειρὶ

ἥρω' "Αδρηστον. τὸν δὲ κρείων 'Αγαμέμνων

οὖτα κατὰ λαπάρην· ὁ δ' ἀνετράπετ', 'Ατρεΐδης δὲ

λὰξ ἐν στήθεσι βὰς ἐξέσπασε μείλινον ἔγχος.   65

Nestor urges on the Greeks. Helenos bids Aineias and
Hektor rally the Trojans, and Hektor to go into Troy
and bid the women pray to Athene.

Νέστωρ δ' 'Αργείοισιν ἐκέκλετο μακρὸν ἀΰσας·

"ὦ φίλοι ἥρωες Δαναοί, θεράποντες "Αρηος,

μή τις νῦν ἐνάρων ἐπιβαλλόμενος μετόπισθεν

μιμνέτω, ὥς κεν πλεῖστα φέρων ἐπὶ νῆας ἵκηται,

ἀλλ' ἄνδρας κτείνωμεν· ἔπειτα δὲ καὶ τὰ ἔκηλοι   70

νεκροὺς ἂμ πεδίον συλήσετε τεθνηῶτας."

ὣς εἰπὼν ὤτρυνε μένος καὶ θυμὸν ἑκάστου.

ἔνθα κεν αὖτε Τρῶες ἀρηιφίλων ὑπ' 'Αχαιῶν

"Ιλιον εἰσανέβησαν ἀναλκείῃσι δαμέντες,

εἰ μὴ ἄρ' Αἰνείᾳ τε καὶ "Εκτορι εἶπε παραστὰς   75

Πριαμίδης "Ελενος, οἰωνοπόλων ὄχ' ἄριστος·

"Αἰνεία τε καὶ "Εκτορ, ἐπεὶ πόνος ὔμμι μάλιστα

58-59   μηδ' ὅν τινα ... ὅς φύγοι: 'may even any baby that a
mother carries in her womb not escape'.
ἐόντα: HF 19E.

60   'Ιλίου: genitive governed by ἐξ in ἐξαπολοίατο.
ἐξαπολοίατο: HF 16.

61   ὣς εἰπών: a common formula, see note on 51.
ἀδελφεόο: HF 5A.

62   Agamemnon's ruthless attitude is typical of him.
ἀπὸ ἕθεν: 'from him', HF 9A note.

63   τόν: HF 20A.

64   οὖτα: 3rd sing. aorist of οὐτάω.
ἀνετράπετ(ο): 'he fell backwards'.

66   μακρὸν ἀύσας: 'with a far-reaching shout'.
Nestor was an old man at the time of the Trojan war.
His main contribution to the cause was giving en-
couragement to the warriors as here, or acting as
counsellor.

68   νῦν: contrasted with ἔπειτα in 70. Nestor says that
the immediate concern is to press on with the killing,
later (ἔπειτα) they can turn their efforts to
collecting loot.

69   ὥς κεν: with subjunctive, 'so that'.

70   καί: 'also'.
τά: HF 20B, i.e. τὰ ἔναρα.

71   συλήσετε: governing two accusatives, τά and νεκρούς.
See note on 17.
ἄμ: HF 2C.

72   ὤτρυνε: 'he began to rouse'.

73   κεν: with εἰσανέβησαν, 'would have gone back into'.

74   ἀναλκείῃσι δαμέντες: 'overcome by their lack of spirit',
HF 4D.

75   Αἰνείᾳ: Aineias, later to become the central hero of
Virgil's Aeneid, plays a comparatively minor role in
Homer's epic.
῞Εκτορι: Hektor is the leading warrior on the Trojan
side.

77   ὕμμι: for ὑμῖν, HF 9A.
μάλιστα with genitive: see vocabulary.

Τρώων καὶ Λυκίων ἐγκέκλιται, οὕνεκ' ἄριστοι

πᾶσαν ἐπ' ἰθύν ἐστε μάχεσθαί τε φρονέειν τε,

στῆτ' αὐτοῦ, καὶ λαὸν ἐρυκάκετε πρὸ πυλάων   80

πάντῃ ἐποιχόμενοι, πρὶν αὖτ' ἐν χερσὶ γυναικῶν

φεύγοντας πεσέειν, δηίοισι δὲ χάρμα γενέσθαι.

αὐτὰρ ἐπεί κε φάλαγγας ἐποτρύνητον ἁπάσας,

ἡμεῖς μὲν Δαναοῖσι μαχησόμεθ' αὖθι μένοντες,

καὶ μάλα τειρόμενοί περ· ἀναγκαίη γὰρ ἐπείγει·   85

Ἕκτορ, ἀτὰρ σὺ πόλινδε μετέρχεο, εἰπὲ δ' ἔπειτα

μητέρι σῇ καὶ ἐμῇ· ἡ δὲ ξυνάγουσα γεραιὰς

νηὸν Ἀθηναίης γλαυκώπιδος ἐν πόλει ἄκρῃ,

οἴξασα κληῖδι θύρας ἱεροῖο δόμοιο,

πέπλον, ὅς οἱ δοκέει χαριέστατος ἠδὲ μέγιστος   90

εἶναι ἐνὶ μεγάρῳ καί οἱ πολὺ φίλτατος αὐτῇ,

θεῖναι Ἀθηναίης ἐπὶ γούνασιν ἠυκόμοιο,

καί οἱ ὑποσχέσθαι δυοκαίδεκα βοῦς ἐνὶ νηῷ

ἤνις ἠκέστας ἱερευσέμεν, αἴ κ' ἐλεήσῃ

ἄστυ τε καὶ Τρώων ἀλόχους καὶ νήπια τέκνα,   95

αἴ κεν Τυδέος υἱὸν ἀπόσχῃ Ἰλίου ἱρῆς,

ἄγριον αἰχμητήν, κρατερὸν μήστωρα φόβοιο,

ὃν δὴ ἐγὼ κάρτιστον Ἀχαιῶν φημὶ γενέσθαι.

οὐδ' Ἀχιλῆά ποθ' ὧδέ γ' ἐδείδιμεν, ὄρχαμον ἀνδρῶν,

ὅν πέρ φασι θεᾶς ἐξ ἔμμεναι· ἀλλ' ὅδε λίην   100

78 ἐγκέκλιται: perfect of ἐγκλίνω, 'rests on'.

79 Both infinitives go with ἄριστοι: 'best both at fighting and planning'.

80 στῆτ' αὐτοῦ: the forceful beginning of this line stresses the urgency of the situation and the need for decisive action.
   πυλάων: HF 4C.

82 χάρμα γενέσθαι: 'and become a source of joy'.

83 ἐποτρύνητον: 2nd pers. dual subj.: 'whenever you have urged on'.

85 καί ... περ: for καίπερ, 'although'.

86 πόλινδε: 'to the city'.
   μετέρχεο, εἰπέ: both imperatives.

87 σῇ καί ἐμῇ: Helenos, the speaker, and Hektor are brothers.

88 νηόν: 'to the temple'. The poet regularly describes the Trojans as worshipping the same gods as the Greeks.

90 οἱ: 'to her'.
   δοκέει: HF 18B.

91 πολύ: adv. 'by far'.
   αὐτῇ: with οἱ for ἑαυτῇ, 'to herself'.

92 θεῖναι: infinitive for imperative, as is ὑποσχέσθαι at 93, '(tell her) to place it'.
   ἠυκόμοιο: compound adjectives usually have no separate feminine forms.

93 οἱ: see note on 90, but here it refers to the goddess.

94 ἱερευσέμεν: this future infinitive depends on ὑποσχέσθαι.
   αἵ κ(ε): 'to see if', 'in the hope that'.

96 Ἰλίου: 'from Ilion'.

97 κρατερόν: HF 2B. The vocalisation of ρ varied between αρ and ρα: see κάρτιστον in 98.

99 ἐδείδιμεν: 'we feared'.

100 ὅν πέρ: 'the very one whom'.
   ἐξ: with θεᾶς.
   ἔμμεναι: HF 19D.
   ὅδε: refers to the son of Tydeus, Diomedes.

μαίνεται, οὐδέ τίς οἱ δύναται μένος ἰσοφαρίζειν."

ὣς ἔφαθ', Ἕκτωρ δ' οὔ τι κασιγνήτῳ ἀπίθησεν.

αὐτίκα δ' ἐξ ὀχέων σὺν τεύχεσιν ἆλτο χαμᾶζε,

πάλλων δ' ὀξέα δοῦρα κατὰ στρατὸν ᾤχετο πάντῃ

ὀτρύνων μαχέσασθαι, ἔγειρε δὲ φύλοπιν αἰνήν.   105

οἱ δ' ἐλελίχθησαν καὶ ἐναντίοι ἔσταν Ἀχαιῶν·

Ἀργεῖοι δ' ὑπεχώρησαν, λῆξαν δὲ φόνοιο,

φὰν δέ τιν' ἀθανάτων ἐξ οὐρανοῦ ἀστερόεντος

Τρωσὶν ἀλεξήσοντα κατελθέμεν· ὣς ἐλέλιχθεν.

Ἕκτωρ δὲ Τρώεσσιν ἐκέκλετο μακρὸν ἀύσας·   110

"Τρῶες ὑπέρθυμοι τηλεκλειτοί τ' ἐπίκουροι,

ἀνέρες ἔστε, φίλοι, μνήσασθε δὲ θούριδος ἀλκῆς,

ὄφρ' ἂν ἐγὼ βήω προτὶ Ἴλιον ἠδὲ γέρουσιν

εἴπω βουλευτῇσι καὶ ἡμετέρῃς ἀλόχοισιν

δαίμοσιν ἀρήσασθαι, ὑποσχέσθαι δ' ἑκατόμβας."   115

ὣς ἄρα φωνήσας ἀπέβη κορυθαίολος Ἕκτωρ·

ἀμφὶ δέ μιν σφυρὰ τύπτε καὶ αὐχένα δέρμα κελαινόν,

ἄντυξ ἣ πυμάτη θέεν ἀσπίδος ὀμφαλοέσσης.

Hektor and Ajax fighting in the presence of Athena
and Apollo; Attic red-figure *kylix*, ca. 475 B.C.;
Louvre, Paris.

101 τίς: the indefinite τις, 'anyone'. The accent comes
    from the enclitic οἱ following it.
    μένος: accusative of respect with ἰσοφαρίζειν, 'in
    strength'.

102 ὣς ἔφαθ': this formula is identical to that in 51 but
    is used because the next word begins with an aspir-
    ated vowel.
    τι: 'in any way'.

104 ὀξέα: HF 6B.
    πάντῃ: 'in every direction'.

105 ἔγειρε: imperfect, 'he kept rousing'.

106 ἐλελίχθησαν: 'they rallied'.
    ἔσταν: for ἔστησαν, 'they stood', HF 12B.

108 φάν: for ἔφασαν, HF 12B, 'they said (to themselves)',
    or 'they thought (to themselves)'.

109 Τρωσίν: with ἀλεξήσοντα.
    κατελθέμεν: HF 17.
    ἐλέλιχθεν: HF 12C.

110 Τρώεσσιν: this form alongside Τρωσίν in 109 illustrates
    the variety of forms an epic poet had at his disposal,
    see Appendix 3.
    μακρὸν ἀύσας: see note on 66.

112 ἀνέρες: HF 6C.
    ἔστε: imperative.

113 ὄφρα ἄν: 'so that'.

114 βουλευτῇσι: HF 4D.

115 ἀρήσασθαι, ὑποσχέσθαι: indirect commands with εἴπω.
    ἑκατόμβας: this word should mean the sacrifice of 100
    oxen, but line 93 clearly shows that it is not to be
    taken literally.

116 ὣς ἄρα φωνήσας: a participial form of the usual form-
    ula. See 61 for a shorter version also with a part-
    iciple.

117 ἀμφί: adverb here, 'covering him', see Appendix 2D.
    μιν σφυρά ... αὐχένα: objects of τύπτε, see note on
    9, 'tapped him on the ankles and neck'. This was
    the large Mycenaean shield which was slung on one's
    back when not in use.

118 ἄντυξ ... θέεν: ἄντυξ used predicatively, 'which
    went as the outer rim ...'.

Diomedes meets Glaukos and enquires about his lineage.

Γλαῦκος δ' ᾽Ιππολόχοιο πάις καὶ Τυδέος υἱὸς

ἐς μέσον ἀμφοτέρων συνίτην μεμαῶτε μάχεσθαι.   120

οἱ δ' ὅτε δὴ σχεδὸν ἦσαν ἐπ' ἀλλήλοισιν ἰόντες,

τὸν πρότερος προσέειπε βοὴν ἀγαθὸς Διομήδης·

"τίς δὲ σύ ἐσσι, φέριστε, καταθνητῶν ἀνθρώπων;

οὐ μὲν γάρ ποτ' ὄπωπα μάχῃ ἔνι κυδιανείρῃ

τὸ πρίν· ἀτὰρ μὲν νῦν γε πολὺ προβέβηκας ἁπάντων   125

σῷ θάρσει, ὅ τ' ἐμὸν δολιχόσκιον ἔγχος ἔμεινας.

δυστήνων δέ τε παῖδες ἐμῷ μένει ἀντιόωσιν.

εἰ δέ τις ἀθανάτων γε κατ' οὐρανοῦ εἰλήλουθας,

οὐκ ἂν ἐγώ γε θεοῖσιν ἐπουρανίοισι μαχοίμην.

οὐδὲ γὰρ οὐδὲ Δρύαντος υἱὸς κρατερὸς Λυκόοργος   130

δὴν ἦν, ὅς ῥα θεοῖσιν ἐπουρανίοισιν ἔριζεν,

ὅς ποτε μαινομένοιο Διωνύσοιο τιθήνας

σεῦε κατ' ἠγάθεον Νυσήιον· αἱ δ' ἅμα πᾶσαι

θύσθλα χαμαὶ κατέχευαν, ὑπ' ἀνδροφόνοιο Λυκούργου

θεινόμεναι βουπλῆγι· Διώνυσος δὲ φοβηθεὶς   135

δύσεθ' ἁλὸς κατὰ κῦμα, Θέτις δ' ὑπεδέξατο κόλπῳ

δειδιότα· κρατερὸς γὰρ ἔχε τρόμος ἀνδρὸς ὁμοκλῇ.

τῷ μὲν ἔπειτ' ὀδύσαντο θεοὶ ῥεῖα ζώοντες,

καί μιν τυφλὸν ἔθηκε Κρόνου πάις· οὐδ' ἄρ' ἔτι δὴν

ἦν, ἐπεὶ ἀθανάτοισιν ἀπήχθετο πᾶσι θεοῖσιν.   140

οὐδ' ἂν ἐγὼ μακάρεσσι θεοῖς ἐθέλοιμι μάχεσθαι.

εἰ δέ τίς ἐσσι βροτῶν, οἳ ἀρούρης καρπὸν ἔδουσιν,

ἆσσον ἴθ', ὥς κεν θᾶσσον ὀλέθρου πείραθ' ἵκηαι."

119 Glaukos was the ξένος or guest-friend of Diomedes.
In Book VII he is described as a leader of the
Lycians, staunch allies of the Trojans.

120 ἐς μέσον ἀμφοτέρων: single combats between the
great warriors usually took place between the two
armies.
μεμαῶτε: nominative dual ending.

122 τόν: refers to Glaukos, HF 20A.

123 ἔσσι: HF 19A.

125 τὸ πρίν: adverbial phrase, 'before this'.

126 ὅ τ(ε): 'in that'. Diomedes explains exactly
what constitutes Glaukos' courage.

127 A threatening comment by Diomedes on the usual fate
of those who oppose him.
ἀντιόωσιν: for ἀντιῶσιν from ἀντιάω, HF 18A.

128 γε: 'in fact'.

130 οὐδέ: repeated for emphasis.
Lykourgos opposed the new orgiastic cult of Dionysos.

131 ἦν: 'lived' or 'survived'.

132 τιθήνας: the nymphs of Mt. Nysa nursed the infant
Dionysos.

137 δειδιότα: refers to Dionysos. With the use of κόλπῳ
and δειδιότα the poet vividly portrays the god in
his terror being comforted like a tiny child.
ἔχε: for εἶχε, 'gripped him'.

138 τῷ: 'with him', i.e. Lykourgos.

139 ἔθηκε: 'made'.

140 ἦν: see note on 131.

142 τίς: see note on 101.

143 ἆσσον: HF 7.
ἴθ': 'come'.
ὥς κεν: see note on 69.
πεῖραθ': from πεῖραρ, 'the end'; ὀλέθρου: '(which con-
sists) of death'
ἵκηαι: HF 15. Regularly followed by accusative.
Heroes usually boasted and antagonised their op-
ponents before a combat.

Glaukos says he is son of Hippolochos, son of the famous Bellerophon, whose story he tells.

τὸν δ' αὖθ' Ἱππολόχοιο προσηύδα φαίδιμος υἱός·

"Τυδείδη μεγάθυμε, τί ἦ γενεὴν ἐρεείνεις;   145

οἵη περ φύλλων γενεή, τοίη δὲ καὶ ἀνδρῶν.

φύλλα τὰ μέν τ' ἄνεμος χαμάδις χέει, ἄλλα δέ θ' ὕλη

τηλεθόωσα φύει, ἔαρος δ' ἐπιγίγνεται ὥρη·

ὣς ἀνδρῶν γενεὴ ἡ μὲν φύει, ἡ δ' ἀπολήγει.

εἰ δ' ἐθέλεις καὶ ταῦτα δαήμεναι, ὄφρ' ἐὺ εἰδῇς   150

ἡμετέρην γενεήν· πολλοὶ δέ μιν ἄνδρες ἴσασιν·

ἔστι πόλις Ἐφύρη μυχῷ Ἄργεος ἱπποβότοιο,

ἔνθα δὲ Σίσυφος ἔσκεν, ὃ κέρδιστος γένετ' ἀνδρῶν,

Σίσυφος Αἰολίδης· ὁ δ' ἄρα Γλαῦκον τέκεθ' υἱόν,

αὐτὰρ Γλαῦκος ἔτικτεν ἀμύμονα Βελλεροφόντην.   155

τῷ δὲ θεοὶ κάλλος τε καὶ ἠνορέην ἐρατεινὴν

ὤπασαν· αὐτάρ οἱ Προῖτος κακὰ μήσατο θυμῷ,

ὅς ῥ' ἐκ δήμου ἔλασσεν, ἐπεὶ πολὺ φέρτερος ἦεν,

Ἀργείων· Ζεὺς γάρ οἱ ὑπὸ σκήπτρῳ ἐδάμασσεν.

τῷ δὲ γυνὴ Προίτου ἐπεμήνατο, δῖ' Ἄντεια,   160

κρυπταδίη φιλότητι μιγήμεναι· ἀλλὰ τὸν οὔ τι

πεῖθ' ἀγαθὰ φρονέοντα, δαΐφρονα Βελλεροφόντην.

Linear B tablet from Knossos; Herakleion
Museum, Crete.

144 τόν: i.e. Diomedes.
αὖθ᾽: 'for his part'.

146 οἵη περ ... τοίη: 'just as ... so', HF 1A.
δέ: called 'apodotic', introduces the main clause
(cf. 475). Supply ἐστί.

147 φύλλα τὰ μέν: 'some leaves ...'.
τ᾽ ... θ᾽: this use of τε, which is not translated,
indicates a sentence of a general or proverbial kind.

148 ἔαρος ... ὥρη: 'as the season of spring comes on'.

149 ὥς: this word marks the application of the simile to
the narrative, 'so', 'in this way'.
ἀνδρῶν γενεὴ ἡ μέν: 'one family of men ...'.
φύει: intrans. here, 'flourishes', cf. 148, where it
is trans.

150 δαήμεναι: HF 17. The apodosis to εἰ ἐθέλεις is post-
poned and becomes Glaukos' story beginning at 152.

151 μιν = αὐτήν, i.e. the family.

152 Ἄργεος: probably used here to denote the whole of the
Peloponnese.

153 ἔσκεν: HF 13.
ὅ: for ὅς, see HF 20C.

157 οἱ: 'against him'.
θυμῷ: 'in his heart'.

158 ἦεν: HF 19B.

159 Ἀργείων: with δήμου in 158.
οἱ: 'his'.
ἐδάμασσεν: supply Ἀργείους as its object.

160 τῷ: i.e. Bellerophon.

161 φιλότητι μιγήμεναι: see note on 25 and HF 17 - the
infinitive depends on ἐπεμήνατο in 160, 'mad enough
to (wish to)'.
οὔ τι: 'not at all'.

162 πεῖθ᾽: for ἔπειθε, HF 10A.

ἡ δὲ ψευσαμένη Προῖτον βασιλῆα προσηύδα·

'τεθναίης, ὦ Προῖτ', ἢ κάκτανε Βελλεροφόντην,

ὅς μ' ἔθελεν φιλότητι μιγήμεναι οὐκ ἐθελούσῃ.'   165

ὣς φάτο, τὸν δὲ ἄνακτα χόλος λάβεν, οἷον ἄκουσεν·

κτεῖναι μέν ῥ' ἀλέεινε, σεβάσσατο γὰρ τό γε θυμῷ,

πέμπε δέ μιν Λυκίηνδε, πόρεν δ' ὅ γε σήματα λυγρά,

γράψας ἐν πίνακι πτυκτῷ θυμοφθόρα πολλά,

δεῖξαι δ' ἠνώγει ᾧ πενθερῷ, ὄφρ' ἀπόλοιτο.   170

αὐτὰρ ὁ βῆ Λυκίηνδε θεῶν ὑπ' ἀμύμονι πομπῇ.

ἀλλ' ὅτε δὴ Λυκίην ἷξε Ξάνθον τε ῥέοντα,

προφρονέως μιν τῖεν ἄναξ Λυκίης εὐρείης·

ἐννῆμαρ ξείνισσε καὶ ἐννέα βοῦς ἱέρευσεν.

ἀλλ' ὅτε δὴ δεκάτη ἐφάνη ῥοδοδάκτυλος Ἠώς,   175

καὶ τότε μιν ἐρέεινε καὶ ᾔτεε σῆμα ἰδέσθαι,

ὅττι ῥά οἱ γαμβροῖο πάρα Προίτοιο φέροιτο.

αὐτὰρ ἐπεὶ δὴ σῆμα κακὸν παρεδέξατο γαμβροῦ,

πρῶτον μέν ῥα Χίμαιραν ἀμαιμακέτην ἐκέλευσεν

πεφνέμεν. ἡ δ' ἄρ' ἔην θεῖον γένος οὐδ' ἀνθρώπων,   180

πρόσθε λέων, ὄπιθεν δὲ δράκων, μέσση δὲ χίμαιρα,

δεινὸν ἀποπνείουσα πυρὸς μένος αἰθομένοιο.

καὶ τὴν μὲν κατέπεφνε θεῶν τεράεσσι πιθήσας·

δεύτερον αὖ Σολύμοισι μαχήσατο κυδαλίμοισιν·

καρτίστην δὴ τήν γε μάχην φάτο δύμεναι ἀνδρῶν.   185

164 τεθναίης: perf. optative of θνήσκω. Almost equiv-
alent to 'you must die'.
κάκτανε: for κατάκτανε, aor. imperative, HF 2C.

165 μ´: for μοι.

166 οἶον ἄκουσεν: 'at hearing such a thing'.

167 τό: HF 20B, refers to the act of killing.
θυμῷ: see note on 157.

168 μιν: HF 9A.
Λυκίηνδε: 'to Lykia'.
σήματα λυγρά: 'fatal signs'.

169 This line has the only reference to writing in Homer.
With the collapse of the Mycenaean Kingdoms, writing
like that on the Linear B tablets vanished. Later
an alphabetic script was taken over from the Phoenicians.
The poet here, by his vague description and lack of detail, adds an air of mystery to the incident.

170 ᾧ: HF 9B.

172 ἷξε: ἵκω, ἱκάνω, ἱκνέομαι take a direct object in
Homer, see note on 143.

174 It was usual to entertain a stranger before question-
ing him about his identity and the reason for his
journey.

176 σῆμα: i.e. the σήματα λυγρά of 168.

177 ὅττι: for ὅ τι, neuter of ὅστις, HF 2A.
πάρα: with γαμβροῖο, see note on ἔπι (15) and Appendix
2B.

179 As often happens in folk tales, the hero is set a series
of tasks and ends by winning the king's daughter and
half his kingdom. Compare Bellerophon with Herakles,
Jason, Theseus etc.

180 ἔην: HF 19B.
ἀνθρώπων: after a repeated γένος.

181 μέσση: HF 2A.

182 δεινόν: adverb.

185 καρτίστην: see note on 97.
μάχην ... δύμεναι: 'plunge into a battle'.

τὸ τρίτον αὖ κατέπεφνεν Ἀμαζόνας ἀντιανείρας.

τῷ δ' ἄρ' ἀνερχομένῳ πυκινὸν δόλον ἄλλον ὕφαινεν·

κρίνας ἐκ Λυκίης εὐρείης φῶτας ἀρίστους

εἷσε λόχον· τοὶ δ' οὔ τι πάλιν οἰκόνδε νέοντο·

πάντας γὰρ κατέπεφνεν ἀμύμων Βελλεροφόντης.   190

ἀλλ' ὅτε δὴ γίγνωσκε θεοῦ γόνον ἠὺν ἐόντα,

αὐτοῦ μιν κατέρυκε, δίδου δ' ὅ γε θυγατέρα ἥν,

δῶκε δέ οἱ τιμῆς βασιληίδος ἥμισυ πάσης·

καὶ μέν οἱ Λύκιοι τέμενος τάμον ἔξοχον ἄλλων,

καλὸν φυταλιῆς καὶ ἀρούρης, ὄφρα νέμοιτο.   195

ἡ δ' ἔτεκε τρία τέκνα δαΐφρονι Βελλεροφόντῃ,

Ἴσανδρόν τε καὶ Ἱππόλοχον καὶ Λαοδάμειαν·

Λαοδάμεια μὲν παρελέξατο μητίετα Ζεύς,

ἡ δ' ἔτεκ' ἀντίθεον Σαρπηδόνα χαλκοκορυστήν.

ἀλλ' ὅτε δὴ καὶ κεῖνος ἀπήχθετο πᾶσι θεοῖσιν,   200

ἦ τοι ὁ κὰπ πεδίον τὸ Ἀλήιον οἶος ἀλᾶτο

ὃν θυμὸν κατέδων, πάτον ἀνθρώπων ἀλεείνων,

Ἴσανδρον δέ οἱ υἱὸν Ἄρης ἆτος πολέμοιο

μαρνάμενον Σολύμοισι κατέκτανε κυδαλίμοισιν,

τὴν δὲ χολωσαμένη χρυσήνιος Ἄρτεμις ἔκτα.   205

Ἱππόλοχος δ' ἔμ' ἔτικτε, καὶ ἐκ τοῦ φημὶ γενέσθαι·

πέμπε δέ μ' ἐς Τροίην, καί μοι μάλα πόλλ' ἐπέτελλεν

αἰὲν ἀριστεύειν καὶ ὑπείροχον ἔμμεναι ἄλλων,

μηδὲ γένος πατέρων αἰσχυνέμεν, οἳ μέγ' ἄριστοι

ἔν τ' Ἐφύρῃ ἐγένοντο καὶ ἐν Λυκίῃ εὐρείῃ.   210

ταύτης τοι γενεῆς τε καὶ αἵματος εὔχομαι εἶναι."

186 'Αμαζόνας: the legendary tribe of warrior women who
lived at the boundaries of the known world. Various
other heroes besides Bellerophon fought them, including Herakles and Theseus.

191 γίγνωσκε: subject is Proitos.
ἐόντα: HF 19E.

192 ἦν: HF 9B and see note on 53.

194 τέμενος: a piece of land set aside for a king or a
god.

195 καλόν: with a repeated τέμενος. The genitives are
descriptive, 'consisting of'.

196 ἡ: i.e. Proitos' daughter, see 192.

198 μητίετα: HF 4A.

199 Sarpedon, like Glaukos his cousin, fought on the Trojan
side. He was killed by Patroklos.

200 κεῖνος: i.e. Bellerophon. The hatred of the gods was
probably incurred when Bellerophon tried to fly to
heaven on the winged horse Pegasos.

201 κάπ: for κατά, HF 2C.
'Αλήιον: this name may mean 'barren wasteland', and
quite possibly a pun is intended with ἀλᾶτο.

202 ὅν: see note on 53 and HF 9B.

203 οἱ: 'his'.

205 τήν: i.e. Laodameia, see 198f.
χρυσήνιος: see note on ἠυκόμοιο (92).
ἔκτα: HF 12B.

208 A concise statement of the heroic ideal. For the
preoccupation of the Homeric heroes with honour and
glory, see the introduction, *The Mycenaean Age
and Homer*.

211 ταύτης τοι γενεῆς: note the emphatic order of words
and the use of the emphatic particle τοι, 'that is
in fact the family ...'.

*Diomedes will not fight with Glaukos. The two swear
friendship.*

ὣς φάτο, γήθησεν δὲ βοὴν ἀγαθὸς Διομήδης.

ἔγχος μὲν κατέπηξεν ἐνὶ χθονὶ πουλυβοτείρῃ,

αὐτὰρ ὁ μειλιχίοισι προσηύδα ποιμένα λαῶν·

"ἦ ῥά νύ μοι ξεῖνος πατρώιός ἐσσι παλαιός·   215

Οἰνεὺς γάρ ποτε δῖος ἀμύμονα Βελλεροφόντην

ξείνισ' ἐνὶ μεγάροισιν ἐείκοσιν ἤματ' ἐρύξας.

οἱ δὲ καὶ ἀλλήλοισι πόρον ξεινήια καλά·

Οἰνεὺς μὲν ζωστῆρα δίδου φοίνικι φαεινόν,

Βελλεροφόντης δὲ χρύσεον δέπας ἀμφικύπελλον,   220

καί μιν ἐγὼ κατέλειπον ἰὼν ἐν δώμασ' ἐμοῖσιν.

Τυδέα δ' οὐ μέμνημαι, ἐπεί μ' ἔτι τυτθὸν ἐόντα

κάλλιφ', ὅτ' ἐν Θήβῃσιν ἀπώλετο λαὸς Ἀχαιῶν.

τῶ νῦν σοὶ μὲν ἐγὼ ξεῖνος φίλος Ἄργεϊ μέσσῳ

εἰμί, σὺ δ' ἐν Λυκίῃ, ὅτε κεν τῶν δῆμον ἵκωμαι.   225

Diomedes and Athena; fragment of a Corinthian votive plaque.

213 πουλυβοτείρῃ: HF 1B.

214 μειλιχίοισι: supply ἐπέεσσι, cf. 337, 'with gentle
words'.

215 The guest-friend (ξεῖνος) was a very important person
in Homeric society. In a land without inns or ho-
tels, such people had a right to protection and
hospitality. This continued into the classical
period: note the anxiety felt by Perikles in 431
B.C. that his guest-friendship with a Spartan king
might cause him political embarrassment (Thuc. 2.13).

216 Oineus was Diomedes' grandfather. Tydeus, his father,
died when Diomedes was young: cf. 222.

218 καί: 'also'.

219 φοίνικι φαεινόν: 'shining with crimson'.

221 μιν: the cup.
ἰών: 'when going away', i.e. when he left for the
Trojan war.

222 ἐόντα: HF 19E.

223 κάλλιφ': HF 2C.
An army led by seven warriors marched from Argos
against Thebes to put Polynikes on the Theban
throne. This expedition, known as the 'Seven
against Thebes', ended in failure and six of the
seven warriors, including Tydeus, were killed.

224 Ἀργεῖ: for ἐν Ἀργεῖ, see note on 152.
μέσσῳ: HF 2A.

225 τῶν: 'their'.
δῆμον: see note on 172.

ἔγχεα δ' ἀλλήλων ἀλεώμεθα καὶ δι' ὁμίλου·

πολλοὶ μὲν γὰρ ἐμοὶ Τρῶες κλειτοί τ' ἐπίκουροι

κτείνειν, ὃν κε θεός γε πόρῃ καὶ ποσσὶ κιχείω,

πολλοὶ δ' αὖ σοὶ 'Αχαιοὶ ἐναιρέμεν, ὃν κε δύνηαι.

τεύχεα δ' ἀλλήλοις ἐπαμείψομεν, ὄφρα καὶ οἴδε   230

γνῶσιν, ὅτι ξεῖνοι πατρώιοι εὐχόμεθ' εἶναι."

    ὣς ἄρα φωνήσαντε καθ' ἵππων ἀίξαντε

χεῖράς τ' ἀλλήλων λαβέτην καὶ πιστώσαντο.

ἔνθ' αὖτε Γλαύκῳ Κρονίδης φρένας ἐξέλετο Ζεύς,

ὃς πρὸς Τυδείδην Διομήδεα τεύχε' ἄμειβεν   235

χρύσεα χαλκείων, ἑκατόμβοι' ἐννεαβοίων.

Hektor comes to Troy where he finds Hekabe. She offers him wine.

῾Έκτωρ δ' ὡς Σκαιάς τε πύλας καὶ φηγὸν ἵκανεν,

ἀμφ' ἄρα μιν Τρώων ἄλοχοι θέον ἠδὲ θύγατρες

εἰρόμεναι παῖδάς τε κασιγνήτους τε ἔτας τε

καὶ πόσιας· ὁ δ' ἔπειτα θεοῖς εὔχεσθαι ἀνώγειν   240

Odysseus attempting to persuade
Achilles to fight; from interior
of wine-cup (*kylix*) by the painter
Douris, ca. 480 B.C.; British
Museum, London.

226 καὶ δι' ὁμίλου: 'even in the throng of battle'.

227 Supply the verb 'to be' with ἐμοί, 'for there are
     many ... for me to kill'.

229 σοί: see previous note on ἐμοί.
     δύνηαι: HF 15.

230 ἐπαμείψομεν: aor. subj., HF 15.

232 ὣς ἄρα φωνήσαντε: another variation of the familiar
     formula, here with a dual ending.
     ἵππων: 'chariot'.
     ἀίξαντε: nom. dual aor. part. act. of ἀίσσω.

233 λαβέτην: 3rd person dual for ἔλαβον.

234 Γλαύκῳ: with φρένας, 'Glaukos' senses'. Note how the
     poet attributes Glaukos' inexplicable behaviour to the
     action of a god. Armour, especially armour of a
     valuable metal, brought honour to its owner and
     enhanced his status. Cf. note on 28.

235 πρός: 'with', cf. such expressions as σπονδὰς
     ποιεῖσθαι πρός τινα.
     ἄμειβεν: followed by an acc. of what is given
     away and a gen. of what is gained in exchange,
     'he exchanged with Diomedes, son of Tydeus,
     golden armour worth 100 oxen for bronze worth
     nine.

237 This line switches our thoughts to Hektor whom we
     left in 118 making his way to the city.
     φηγόν: the oak, like the fig tree of 433, is a
     conspicuous part of the scenery of the Trojan
     plain in the Iliad.

238 θέον: from θέω, 'they came running' (imperfect).

Funeral games; from the Francois Vase, an early sixth century B.C. black-figure volute crater painted by Kleitias.

πάσας ἐξείης·   πολλῆσι δὲ κήδε᾿ ἐφῆπτο.

ἀλλ᾿ ὅτε δὴ Πριάμοιο δόμον περικαλλέ᾿ ἵκανεν,

ξεστῆς αἰθούσῃσι τετυγμένον, αὐτὰρ ἐν αὐτῷ

πεντήκοντ᾿ ἔνεσαν θάλαμοι ξεστοῖο λίθοιο,

πλησίον ἀλλήλων δεδμημένοι· ἔνθα δὲ παῖδες   245

κοιμῶντο Πριάμοιο παρὰ μνηστῇς ἀλόχοισιν·

κουράων δ᾿ ἑτέρωθεν ἐναντίοι ἔνδοθεν αὐλῆς

δώδεκ᾿ ἔσαν τέγεοι θάλαμοι ξεστοῖο λίθοιο,

πλησίον ἀλλήλων δεδμημένοι· ἔνθα δὲ γαμβροὶ

κοιμῶντο Πριάμοιο παρ᾿ αἰδοίης ἀλόχοισιν.   250

ἔνθα οἱ ἠπιόδωρος ἐναντίη ἤλυθε μήτηρ

Λαοδίκην ἐσάγουσα, θυγατρῶν εἶδος ἀρίστην·

ἔν τ᾿ ἄρα οἱ φῦ χειρί, ἔπος τ᾿ ἔφατ᾿ ἔκ τ᾿ ὀνόμαζεν·

"τέκνον, τίπτε λιπὼν πόλεμον θρασὺν εἰλήλουθας;

ἦ μάλα δὴ τείρουσι δυσώνυμοι υἷες ᾿Αχαιῶν   255

μαρνάμενοι περὶ ἄστυ, σὲ δ᾿ ἐνθάδε θυμὸς ἀνῆκεν

ἐλθόντ᾿ ἐξ ἄκρης πόλιος Διὶ χεῖρας ἀνασχεῖν.

ἀλλὰ μέν᾿, ὄφρα κέ τοι μελιηδέα οἶνον ἐνείκω,

ὡς σπείσῃς Διὶ πατρὶ καὶ ἄλλοις ἀθανάτοισιν

πρῶτον, ἔπειτα δὲ καὐτὸς ὀνήσεαι, αἴ κε πίῃσθα.   260

ἀνδρὶ δὲ κεκμηῶτι μένος μέγα οἶνος ἀέξει,

ὡς τύνη κέκμηκας ἀμύνων σοῖσιν ἔτῃσιν."

241 κήδε᾽ ἐφῆπτο: 'sorrows were brought to ...'.

244 ἔνεσαν: HF 19B.

247 κουράων: HF 4C, with θάλαμοι in next line, 'rooms
of his daughters'.

251 οἱ: i.e. Hektor, subject of ἵκανεν (237).

252 εἶδος: acc. defining ἀρίστην, 'best in appearance'.

253 ἐν: tmesis, ἐν ... φῦ χειρί, 'she grasped his hand'
(ἐμφύομαι).
ἐκ: tmesis also, ἐκ ... ὀνόμαζεν for ἐξονόμαζεν,
see Appendix 2C.

256 ἐνθάδε: with ἐλθόντα in 257.

257 ἐξ ἄκρης πόλιος: with ἀνασχεῖν.
πόλιος: gen. of πόλις, HF 6C.

258 μέν(ε):   2nd sing. pres. imperative.
τοι: for σοι, HF 9A.

260 ὀνήσεαι and πίῃσθα: HF 15.
αἴ κε: 'whenever'.

261 μέγα: adverb, 'greatly'.

Bronze dagger studded with gold nails and
decorated with silver and gold inlay, de-
picting a lion-hunt in which the hunters
carry figure-of-eight and tall 'body-
shields'.   From Shaft Grave IV at Mycenae;
National Museum, Athens.

Hektor will not drink. He tells his mother to pray to Athene.

τὴν δ' ἠμείβετ' ἔπειτα μέγας κορυθαίολος Ἕκτωρ·

"μή μοι οἶνον ἄειρε μελίφρονα, πότνια μῆτερ,

μή μ' ἀπογυιώσῃς μένεος, ἀλκῆς τε λάθωμαι·   265

χερσὶ δ' ἀνίπτοισιν Διὶ λείβειν αἴθοπα οἶνον

ἄζομαι· οὐδέ πῃ ἔστι κελαινεφέι Κρονίωνι

αἵματι καὶ λύθρῳ πεπαλαγμένον εὐχετάασθαι.

ἀλλὰ σὺ μὲν πρὸς νηὸν 'Αθηναίης ἀγελείης

ἔρχεο σὺν θυέεσσιν, ἀολλίσσασα γεραιάς·   270

πέπλον δ', ὅς τίς τοι χαριέστατος ἠδὲ μέγιστος

ἔστιν ἐνὶ μεγάρῳ καί τοι πολὺ φίλτατος αὐτῇ,

τὸν θὲς 'Αθηναίης ἐπὶ γούνασιν ἠυκόμοιο,

καί οἱ ὑποσχέσθαι δυοκαίδεκα βοῦς ἐνὶ νηῷ

ἤνις ἠκέστας ἱερευσέμεν, αἴ κ' ἐλεήσῃ   275

ἄστυ τε καὶ Τρώων ἀλόχους καὶ νήπια τέκνα,

αἴ κεν Τυδέος υἱὸν ἀπόσχῃ 'Ιλίου ἱρῆς,

ἄγριον αἰχμητήν, κρατερὸν μήστωρα φόβοιο.

ἀλλὰ σὺ μὲν πρὸς νηὸν 'Αθηναίης ἀγελείης

ἔρχευ, ἐγὼ δὲ Πάριν μετελεύσομαι, ὄφρα καλέσσω,   280

αἴ κ' ἐθέλῃσ' εἰπόντος ἀκουέμεν· ὥς κέ οἱ αὖθι

γαῖα χάνοι· μέγα γάρ μιν 'Ολύμπιος ἔτρεφε πῆμα

Τρωσί τε καὶ Πριάμῳ μεγαλήτορι τοῖό τε παισίν.

εἰ κεῖνόν γε ἴδοιμι κατελθόντ' "Αιδος εἴσω,

φαίην κεν φίλον ἦτορ ὀιζύος ἐκλελαθέσθαι."   285

265   μή ... μένεος: 'lest you sap my knees of strength'.

266   Washing, if only ritual washing, was a necessity before any religious activity.

267   ἔστι: 'it is possible'.

271-278   See 90-97. The poet has only made those changes which are necessary for the sense. Otherwise, Helenos' instructions are repeated word for word. See Appendix 3.

272   αὐτῇ: with τοι, 'to yourself'.

273   τόν: 'that one'.

279   ἀλλά: repeated here for emphasis from 269.

280   ἔρχευ: HF 18B.

281   ἐθέλησ(ι): HF 15.
εἰπόντος: supply ἐμοῦ, 'to listen to me talking to him'.
ὥς κε ... χάνοι: it is unusual to find κε used in a wish, 'how I wish that the earth would open up and swallow him on the spot (αὖθι)'.

282   μέγα ... πῆμα: in predicative sense, 'to be a great cause of sorrow to'.

283   τοῖο: 'his', i.e. Priam's.

284   Ἄιδος εἴσω: supply δόμον, 'into the house of Hades'.

285   φαίην κεν ... ἐκλελαθέσθαι: 'I would say that my own heart had forgotten its distress'. Instead of φίλον ἦτορ MSS have φρέν' ἀτέρπου or φρέν' ἀτερπον. However, since ἀτερπος does not seem to be a Homeric form, Zenodotus' suggested reading has been adopted here.

Blinding of Polyphemus; from Caeretan water-jug (hydria), ca. 520 B.C.; Villa Giulia, Rome.

Hekabe prays to Athene in the temple of the Goddess.

ὣς ἔφαθ', ἡ δὲ μολοῦσα ποτὶ μέγαρ' ἀμφιπόλοισιν

κέκλετο· ταὶ δ' ἄρ' ἀόλλισσαν κατὰ ἄστυ γεραιάς.

αὐτὴ δ' ἐς θάλαμον κατεβήσετο κηώεντα,

ἔνθ' ἔσαν οἱ πέπλοι παμποίκιλοι, ἔργα γυναικῶν

Σιδονίων, τὰς αὐτὸς Ἀλέξανδρος θεοειδὴς   290

ἤγαγε Σιδονίηθεν, ἐπιπλὼς εὑρέα πόντον,

τὴν ὁδόν, ἣν Ἑλένην περ ἀνήγαγεν εὐπατέρειαν.

τῶν ἕν' ἀειραμένη Ἑκάβη φέρε δῶρον Ἀθήνῃ,

ὃς κάλλιστος ἔην ποικίλμασιν ἠδὲ μέγιστος,

ἀστὴρ δ' ὣς ἀπέλαμπεν· ἔκειτο δὲ νείατος ἄλλων.   295

βῆ δ' ἰέναι, πολλαὶ δὲ μετεσσεύοντο γεραιαί.

αἱ δ' ὅτε νηὸν ἵκανον Ἀθήνης ἐν πόλει ἄκρῃ,

τῇσι θύρας ᾦξε Θεανὼ καλλιπάρῃος,

Κισσηίς, ἄλοχος Ἀντήνορος ἱπποδάμοιο·

τὴν γὰρ Τρῶες ἔθηκαν Ἀθηναίης ἱέρειαν.   300

αἱ δ' ὀλολυγῇ πᾶσαι Ἀθήνῃ χεῖρας ἀνέσχον·

ἡ δ' ἄρα πέπλον ἑλοῦσα Θεανὼ καλλιπάρῃος

θῆκεν Ἀθηναίης ἐπὶ γούνασιν ἠυκόμοιο,

εὐχομένη δ' ἠρᾶτο Διὸς κούρῃ μεγάλοιο·

"πότνι' Ἀθηναίη, ῥυσίπτολι, δῖα θεάων,   305

ἄξον δὴ ἔγχος Διομήδεος, ἠδὲ καὶ αὐτὸν

πρηνέα δὸς πεσέειν Σκαιῶν προπάροιθε πυλάων,

ὄφρα τοι αὐτίκα νῦν δυοκαίδεκα βοῦς ἐνὶ νηῷ

ἤνις ἠκέστας ἱερεύσομεν, αἴ κ' ἐλεήσῃς

ἄστυ τε καὶ Τρώων ἀλόχους καὶ νήπια τέκνα."   310

ὣς ἔφατ' εὐχομένη, ἀνένευε δὲ Παλλὰς Ἀθήνη.

290   Sidon, one of the chief cities of the Phoenicians,
     was famous for its production and export of
     purple cloth.
     τάς: HF 20C.

292   τὴν ὁδόν, ἥν ... περ: 'on that very journey when ...'.
     ὁδόν is a second object of the cognate type following
     ἐπιπλώς.

293   τῶν: 'of these', i.e. πέπλοι (289).

295   ἀστὴρ δ' ὥς: 'like a star'.
     νείατος ἄλλων: 'lowest of all'.

296   βῆ δ' ἰέναι: 'she hastened to go'.

298   τῇσι: 'for them', i.e. the old women.
     καλλιπάρῃος: see note on 92.
     Theano the priestess was daughter of Kisseus, king of
       Thrace. The three sons of Theano and Antenor met
       their death in battle at the hands of Agamemnon
       (*Iliad* XI 221ff.).

305   δῖα θεάων: 'glorious among goddesses'.

306-7 καὶ αὐτόν ... δός: 'and grant that he ...'.

309   ἱερεύσομεν: aor. subj., HF 15, 'so that we may
     sacrifice'.

311   Nodding the head upwards was the sign of refusal
     and nodding downwards (κατανεύω) was the sign for
     assent.
     Prayers to gods in Homer may be granted, partially
     granted or (as here) refused; the god's reaction
     bears no necessary relationship to the merit of
     the request or of the person making it.

Paris fleeing from Menelaus; from an early fifth
century B.C. wine-cup (*kylix*) by Douris.

44

ὣς αἱ μέν ῥ᾽ εὔχοντο Διὸς κούρῃ μεγάλοιο,
Ἕκτωρ δὲ πρὸς δώματ᾽ Ἀλεξάνδροιο βεβήκειν
καλά, τά ῥ᾽ αὐτὸς ἔτευξε σὺν ἀνδράσιν, οἳ τότ᾽ ἄριστοι
ἦσαν ἐνὶ Τροίῃ ἐριβώλακι τέκτονες ἄνδρες·   315
οἵ οἱ ἐποίησαν θάλαμον καὶ δῶμα καὶ αὐλὴν
ἐγγύθι τε Πριάμοιο καὶ Ἕκτορος ἐν πόλει ἄκρῃ.
ἔνθ᾽ Ἕκτωρ εἰσῆλθε διίφιλος, ἐν δ᾽ ἄρα χειρὶ
ἔγχος ἔχ᾽ ἑνδεκάπηχυ· πάροιθε δὲ λάμπετο δουρὸς
αἰχμὴ χαλκείη, περὶ δὲ χρύσεος θέε πόρκης.   320
τὸν δ᾽ εὗρ᾽ ἐν θαλάμῳ περικαλλέα τεύχε᾽ ἔποντα,
ἀσπίδα καὶ θώρηκα καὶ ἀγκύλα τόξ᾽ ἀφόωντα·
Ἀργείη δ᾽ Ἑλένη μετ᾽ ἄρα δμῳῇσι γυναιξὶν
ἧστο καὶ ἀμφιπόλοισι περικλυτὰ ἔργα κέλευεν.
τὸν δ᾽ Ἕκτωρ νείκεσσεν ἰδὼν αἰσχροῖς ἐπέεσσιν·   325
"δαιμόνι᾽, οὐ μὲν καλὰ χόλον τόνδ᾽ ἔνθεο θυμῷ.
λαοὶ μὲν φθινύθουσι περὶ πτόλιν αἰπύ τε τεῖχος
μαρνάμενοι· σέο δ᾽ εἵνεκ᾽ ἀυτή τε πτόλεμός τε
ἄστυ τόδ᾽ ἀμφιδέδηε· σὺ δ᾽ ἂν μαχέσαιο καὶ ἄλλῳ,
ὅν τινά που μεθιέντα ἴδοις στυγεροῦ πολέμοιο.   330
ἀλλ᾽ ἄνα, μὴ τάχα ἄστυ πυρὸς δηίοιο θέρηται."
    τὸν δ᾽ αὖτε προσέειπεν Ἀλέξανδρος θεοειδής·
"Ἕκτορ, ἐπεί με κατ᾽ αἶσαν ἐνείκεσας οὐδ᾽ ὑπὲρ αἶσαν,
τοὔνεκά τοι ἐρέω· σὺ δὲ σύνθεο καί μευ ἄκουσον.
οὔ τοι ἐγὼ Τρώων τόσσον χόλῳ οὐδὲ νεμέσσι   335

314 καλά: 'beautiful', with δώματα.
τά: HF 20C.
αὐτός: i.e. Alexander.

316 This line gives the three main parts of a Homeric
house: θάλαμος, bedroom; δῶμα, main living-room
(sometimes called μέγαρον); and αὐλή, courtyard.

317 ἐγγύθι ... Ἕκτορος: 'near those of Priam and Hektor'.
From this we must suppose that Paris and Hektor
lived outside the palace and are not included with
Priam's sons in 245-6.

319 ἐχ': for εἶχε.
πάροιθε: adverb, 'in front (of him) gleamed the
bronze spear-tip'.

320 περὶ δέ ... θέε: tmesis, 'and around it ran'.

321 τόν: i.e. Alexander.

324 ἀμφιπόλοισι: these are the δμωῇσι γυναιξίν of the
previous line.
κέλευεν: here the dat. of person ordered and acc.
of thing ordered, 'she was ordering excellent pieces
of work from her servants'. The ἔργα would have been
the products of spinning and weaving.

325 τόν: see note on 321.
αἰσχροῖς ἐπέεσσιν: i.e. 'words bringing shame (to the
hearer)'

326 δαιμόνι(ε): always in the voc., 'my dear man'. Used
when someone is remonstrating with another: the im-
plication is that the person concerned is acting under
the influence of a spirit (δαίμων).
οὐ ... θυμῷ: καλά is adverbial, 'it's not good that
you have stored up this anger in your heart'. The
anger, as Paris explains in 335-6, is not against
the Trojans but at himself for losing his combat
with Menelaos.

328 σέο: HF 9A.

329 καὶ ἄλλῳ: 'also with anyone else'.

331 ἀλλ': with imperative, to encourage and persuade, 'well
now'.
ἄνα: adverb used as imperative: '(get) up'.
μή: 'lest'.
πυρὸς δηΐοιο θέρηται: 'may burn with fire from the enemy'.

333-35 Notes on these lines are on p.47.

ἤμην ἐν θαλάμῳ, ἔθελον δ' ἀχεῖ προτραπέσθαι.

νῦν δέ με παρειποῦσ' ἄλοχος μαλακοῖς ἐπέεσσιν

ὥρμησ' ἐς πόλεμον, δοκέει δέ μοι ὧδε καὶ αὐτῷ

λώιον ἔσσεσθαι· νίκη δ' ἐπαμείβεται ἄνδρας.

ἀλλ' ἄγε νῦν ἐπίμεινον, ἀρήια τεύχεα δύω·   340

ἢ ἴθ', ἐγὼ δὲ μέτειμι, κιχήσεσθαι δέ σ' ὀίω."

Helen bemoans her ruinous life and speaks slightingly
of Paris. Hektor will not stay to talk with her.

ὣς φάτο, τὸν δ' οὔ τι προσέφη κορυθαίολος Ἕκτωρ·

τὸν δ' Ἑλένη μύθοισι προσηύδα μειλιχίοισιν·

"δᾶερ ἐμεῖο, κυνὸς κακομηχάνοο κρυοέσσης,

ὥς μ' ὄφελ' ἤματι τῷ, ὅτε με πρῶτον τέκε μήτηρ,   345

οἴχεσθαι προφέρουσα κακὴ ἀνέμοιο θύελλα

εἰς ὄρος ἢ εἰς κῦμα πολυφλοίσβοιο θαλάσσης,

ἔνθα με κῦμ' ἀπόερσε πάρος τάδε ἔργα γενέσθαι.

αὐτὰρ ἐπεὶ τάδε γ' ὧδε θεοὶ κακὰ τεκμήραντο,

ἀνδρὸς ἔπειτ' ὤφελλον ἀμείνονος εἶναι ἄκοιτις,   350

ὃς ᾔδη νέμεσίν τε καὶ αἴσχεα πόλλ' ἀνθρώπων.

τούτῳ δ' οὔτ' ἄρ νῦν φρένες ἔμπεδοι οὔτ' ἄρ' ὀπίσσω

ἔσσονται· τῶ καί μιν ἐπαυρήσεσθαι ὀίω.

ἀλλ' ἄγε νῦν εἴσελθε καὶ ἕζεο τῷδ' ἐπὶ δίφρῳ,

δᾶερ, ἐπεί σε μάλιστα πόνος φρένας ἀμφιβέβηκεν   355

εἵνεκ' ἐμεῖο κυνὸς καὶ Ἀλεξάνδρου ἕνεκ' ἄτης,

οἷσιν ἐπὶ Ζεὺς θῆκε κακὸν μόρον, ὡς καὶ ὀπίσσω

ἀνθρώποισι πελώμεθ' ἀοίδιμοι ἐσσομένοισιν."

333   κατ' αἶσαν: 'according to my deserts', 'rightly'.
       ὑπὲρ αἶσαν: 'beyond my deserts', 'unfairly'.

334   μευ: HF 9A.

335   τοι: emphatic particle, 'in fact'.
       Τρώων ... νεμέσσι: νεμέσσι is dat. sing. of νέμεσις,
       'not so much in anger and annoyance at the Trojans'.

338   καί: is usually used with αὐτός meaning 'self'.

339   ἐπαμείβεται ἄνδρας: 'goes round in turn from man
       to man'.

340   δύω: subjunctive, 'let me put on'.

344   ἐμεῖο: HF 9A.
       κακομηχάνοο: HF 5A.

345   ὡς: introducing a wish, ὥς μ' ὄφελ' ... θύελλα: 'a
       storm ... should have ...'.
       τῷ: HF 20B.

348   ἀπόερσε: supply ἄν, 'would have swept me away'.
       πάρος: here used like πρίν and infinitive.

350   ἔπειτ' ὤφελλον ... εἶναι: 'then I should have been'.

352   τούτῳ: i.e. Alexander.

353   μιν: subject of the infinitive.

355   σε ... φρένας: see note on ἔβαλε (9).

356   εἵνεκ' ... ἕνεκ': illustrates the metrical variety
       in forms available to the poet.

357   ἐπί: not with οἶσιν (note the accent) but an example
       of tmesis.

358   ἀοίδιμοι ἐσσομένοισι: 'the subjects of songs for
       people in the future'.

τὴν δ᾽ ἠμείβετ᾽ ἔπειτα μέγας κορυθαίολος Ἕκτωρ·

"μή με κάθιζ᾽, Ἑλένη, φιλέουσά περ· οὐδέ με πείσεις· 360

ἤδη γάρ μοι θυμὸς ἐπέσσυται, ὄφρ᾽ ἐπαμύνω

Τρώεσσ᾽, οἳ μέγ᾽ ἐμεῖο ποθὴν ἀπεόντος ἔχουσιν.

ἀλλὰ σύ γ᾽ ὄρνυθι τοῦτον, ἐπειγέσθω δὲ καὶ αὐτός,

ὥς κεν ἔμ᾽ ἔντοσθεν πόλιος καταμάρψῃ ἐόντα.

καὶ γὰρ ἐγὼν οἴκόνδε ἐλεύσομαι, ὄφρα ἴδωμαι 365

οἰκῆας ἄλοχόν τε φίλην καὶ νήπιον υἰόν·

οὐ γάρ τ᾽ οἶδ᾽, ἦ ἔτι σφιν ὑπότροπος ἵξομαι αὖτις,

ἦ ἤδη μ᾽ ὑπὸ χερσὶ θεοὶ δαμόωσιν Ἀχαιῶν."

Hektor looks for his wife Andromache in their house, but
she has gone to the town wall with her child.

ὣς ἄρα φωνήσας ἀπέβη κορυθαίολος Ἕκτωρ.

αἶψα δ᾽ ἔπειθ᾽ ἵκανε δόμους ἐὺ ναιετάοντας, 370

οὐδ᾽ εὗρ᾽ Ἀνδρομάχην λευκώλενον ἐν μεγάροισιν,

ἀλλ᾽ ἥ γε ξὺν παιδὶ καὶ ἀμφιπόλῳ ἐυπέπλῳ

πύργῳ ἐφεστήκει γοόωσά τε μυρομένη τε.

Ἕκτωρ δ᾽ ὡς οὐκ ἔνδον ἀμύμονα τέτμεν ἄκοιτιν,

ἔστη ἐπ᾽ οὐδὸν ἰών, μετὰ δὲ δμωῇσιν ἔειπεν· 375

"εἰ δ᾽ ἄγε μοι, δμωαί, νημερτέα μυθήσασθε·

πῇ ἔβη Ἀνδρομάχη λευκώλενος ἐκ μεγάροιο;

ἠέ πῃ ἐς γαλόων ἢ εἰνατέρων ἐυπέπλων,

ἦ ἐς Ἀθηναίης ἐξοίχεται, ἔνθα περ ἄλλαι

Τρωαὶ ἐυπλόκαμοι δεινὴν θεὸν ἰλάσκονται;" 380

361 ἐπέσσυται: a perfect tense, 'is eager'.

367 The poet hints that Hektor's death is imminent.
σφιν: HF 9A.

370 ἐὺ ναιετάοντας: 'well-appointed' or 'comfortable'.

372 γε: 'in fact'.

375 ἐπ᾽ οὐδὸν ἰών: 'going to the threshold', i.e. Hektor
did not enter the women's quarters.
μετά: see note on ἐπί (357).

376 εἰ δ᾽ ἄγε: an exclamation, cf. ἄγε in 340 and 354,
'come now, maids'.

378 ἐς γαλόων ἠ εἰνατέρων: supply δόμον. Both γαλόων
and εἰνατέρων were sisters-in-law, the former
being sisters of one's husband, the latter wives
of one's brothers.

379 ἐς Ἀθηναίης: supply νηόν.

Hektor chiding Paris; an engraving of a drawing by Flaxman,
from *The Iliad of Homer Engraved from the Compositions of
John Flaxman*, Longman, 1805.

τὸν δ' αὖτ' ὀτρηρὴ ταμίη πρὸς μῦθον ἔειπεν·

""Εκτορ, ἐπεὶ μάλ' ἄνωγας ἀληθέα μυθήσασθαι,

οὔτε πη ἐς γαλόων οὔτ' εἰνατέρων ἐυπέπλων

οὔτ' ἐς 'Αθηναίης ἐξοίχεται, ἔνθα περ ἄλλαι

Τρωαὶ ἐυπλόκαμοι δεινὴν θεὸν ἱλάσκονται,   385

ἀλλ' ἐπὶ πύργον ἔβη μέγαν 'Ιλίου, οὕνεκ' ἄκουσεν

τείρεσθαι Τρῶας, μέγα δὲ κράτος εἶναι 'Αχαιῶν.

ἡ μὲν δὴ πρὸς τεῖχος ἐπειγομένη ἀφικάνει

μαινομένη ἐικυῖα· φέρει δ' ἅμα παῖδα τιθήνη."

Hektor meets Andromache. She begs him to stay away from the battle, lest she be made a widow and their baby an orphan.

ἣ ῥα γυνὴ ταμίη, ὁ δ' ἀπέσσυτο δώματος "Εκτωρ   390

τὴν αὐτὴν ὁδὸν αὖτις ἐυκτιμένας κατ' ἀγυιάς.

εὖτε πύλας ἵκανε διερχόμενος μέγα ἄστυ,

Σκαιάς, τῇ ἄρ' ἔμελλε διεξίμεναι πεδίονδε,

ἔνθ' ἄλοχος πολύδωρος ἐναντίη ἦλθε θέουσα

'Ανδρομάχη, θυγάτηρ μεγαλήτορος 'Ηετίωνος,   395

'Ηετίων, ὃς ἔναιεν ὑπὸ Πλάκῳ ὑληέσσῃ,

Θήβῃ ὑποπλακίῃ, Κιλίκεσσ' ἀνδρεσσιν ἀνάσσων·

τοῦ περ δὴ θυγάτηρ ἔχεθ' "Εκτορι χαλκοκορυστῇ.

ἥ οἱ ἔπειτ' ἤντησ', ἅμα δ' ἀμφίπολος κίεν αὐτῇ

παῖδ' ἐπὶ κόλπῳ ἔχουσ' ἀταλάφρονα, νήπιον αὔτως   400

'Εκτορίδην ἀγαπητόν, ἀλίγκιον ἀστέρι καλῷ,

τὸν ῥ' "Εκτωρ καλέεσκε Σκαμάνδριον, αὐτὰρ οἱ ἄλλοι

'Αστυάνακτ'· οἶος γὰρ ἐρύετο "Ιλιον "Εκτωρ.

381 αὖτ': 'in reply'.

383 The poet often repeats verbatim what someone has
said previously, see 90-97 and 271-278.

390 ἦ: a verbal form, 'she spoke'.

391 τὴν αὐτὴν ὁδόν: internal accus. with ἀπέσσυτο, 'along
the same route'.
αὖτις: 'back again'. This makes it clear that Hektor
is retracing his own steps and not going the same way
as Andromache.
κατ(ά): here implies purpose, '(so as to come) down
to'.

393 τῇ: supply ὁδῷ, 'the way by which'.

394 πολύδωρος: the giving of gifts was an important feature
of a marriage in Homeric society. Suitors brought
gifts for the girl's parents and the bride brought
a dowry with her. The size and/or value of these
gifts and of the dowry were an indication of the
prestige of the people concerned.

399 ἅμα: here a preposition with αὐτῇ.

400 νήπιον αὔτως: 'only an infant'.

402 καλέεσκε: 'he used to call', HF 13.

Nestor talking to Odysseus; from
interior of wine-cup (kylix) by the
Brygos Painter, ca. 490 B.C.;
Kunsthistorisches Museum, Vienna.

ἦ τοι ὁ μὲν μείδησεν ἰδὼν ἐς παῖδα σιωπῇ·

Ἀνδρομάχη δέ οἱ ἄγχι παρίστατο δάκρυ χέουσα,   405

ἔν τ᾽ ἄρα οἱ φῦ χειρί, ἔπος τ᾽ ἔφατ᾽ ἔκ τ᾽ ὀνόμαζεν·

"δαιμόνιε, φθίσει σε τὸ σὸν μένος, οὐδ᾽ ἐλεαίρεις

παῖδά τε νηπίαχον καὶ ἔμ᾽ ἄμμορον, ἣ τάχα χήρη

σεῦ ἔσομαι· τάχα γάρ σε κατακτανέουσιν Ἀχαιοὶ

πάντες ἐφορμηθέντες· ἐμοὶ δέ κε κέρδιον εἴη   410

σεῦ ἀφαμαρτούσῃ χθόνα δύμεναι· οὐ γὰρ ἔτ᾽ ἄλλη

ἔσται θαλπωρή, ἐπεὶ ἂν σύ γε πότμον ἐπίσπῃς,

ἀλλ᾽ ἄχε᾽· οὐδέ μοι ἔστι πατὴρ καὶ πότνια μήτηρ.

ἦ τοι γὰρ πατέρ᾽ ἁμὸν ἀπέκτανε δῖος Ἀχιλλεύς,

ἐκ δὲ πόλιν πέρσεν Κιλίκων ἐῢ ναιετόωσαν,   415

Θήβην ὑψίπυλον· κατὰ δ᾽ ἔκτανεν Ἠετίωνα,

οὐδέ μιν ἐξενάριξε, σεβάσσατο γὰρ τό γε θυμῷ,

ἀλλ᾽ ἄρα μιν κατέκηε σὺν ἔντεσι δαιδαλέοισιν

ἠδ᾽ ἐπὶ σῆμ᾽ ἔχεεν· περὶ δὲ πτελέας ἐφύτευσαν

νύμφαι ὀρεστιάδες, κοῦραι Διὸς αἰγιόχοιο.   420

οἳ δέ μοι ἑπτὰ κασίγνητοι ἔσαν ἐν μεγάροισιν,

οἱ μὲν πάντες ἰῷ κίον ἤματι Ἄιδος εἴσω·

πάντας γὰρ κατέπεφνε ποδάρκης δῖος Ἀχιλλεὺς

βουσὶν ἐπ᾽ εἰλιπόδεσσι καὶ ἀργεννῇς ὀίεσσιν.

μητέρα δ᾽, ἣ βασίλευεν ὑπὸ Πλάκῳ ὑληέσσῃ,   425

τὴν ἐπεὶ ἂρ δεῦρ᾽ ἤγαγ᾽ ἅμ᾽ ἄλλοισι κτεάτεσσιν,

ἂψ ὅ γε τὴν ἀπέλυσε λαβὼν ἀπερείσι᾽ ἄποινα,

πατρὸς δ᾽ ἐν μεγάροισι βάλ᾽ Ἄρτεμις ἰοχέαιρα.

Ἕκτορ, ἀτὰρ σύ μοί ἐσσι πατὴρ καὶ πότνια μήτηρ

ἠδὲ κασίγνητος, σὺ δέ μοι θαλερὸς παρακοίτης·   430

404 ὁ μέν: i.e. Hektor.

405 οἱ: with παρίστατο (ἄγχι is adverbial here).

406 The regular formula for two people meeting, see also
253.

407 δαιμόνιε: see note on 326.
φθίσει ... μένος: note the repeated menacing σ
sound in this phrase.

409 σεῦ: HF 9A.
κατακτανέουσιν: future tense.

414 ἀμόν: HF 9B.

417 οὐδέ: 'but he did not'.
τό: 'this', HF 20B.

418 To allow an enemy to be cremated in his armour was
a mark of great respect. For the value of armour
and its ability to confer status see notes on 234-
236.

419 ἐπί and περί: probably adverbial uses here, see
Appendix 2D.
σῆμ(α): here clearly a mound is meant.

422 ἰῷ: neuter dat. of the number 'one', HF 8.
Ἄιδος: see note on 284.

424 ἐπ(ί): 'in charge of'. A sad and inglorious end,
not death in battle but slaughtered among the
animals.

426 κτεάτεσσιν: enslaved captives are meant.

428 πατρός: i.e. her mother's father not Andromache's
own father. Andromache's mother returned to her
own family since her husband had been killed.

Funeral scene; from large grave-marker vase (*amphora*), ca. 750 B.C.;
National Museum, Athens.

ἀλλ' ἄγε νῦν ἐλέαιρε καὶ αὐτοῦ μίμν' ἐπὶ πύργῳ,
μὴ παῖδ' ὀρφανικὸν θήῃς χήρην τε γυναῖκα·
λαὸν δὲ στῆσον παρ' ἐρινεόν, ἔνθα μάλιστα
ἀμβατός ἐστι πόλις καὶ ἐπίδρομον ἔπλετο τεῖχος·
τρὶς γὰρ τῇ γ' ἐλθόντες ἐπειρήσανθ' οἱ ἄριστοι   435
ἀμφ' Αἴαντε δύω καὶ ἀγακλυτὸν Ἰδομενῆα
ἠδ' ἀμφ' Ἀτρεΐδας καὶ Τυδέος ἄλκιμον υἱόν·
ἦ πού τίς σφιν ἔνισπε θεοπροπίων ἐὺ εἰδώς,
ἦ νυ καὶ αὐτῶν θυμὸς ἐποτρύνει καὶ ἀνώγει."

    τὴν δ' αὖτε προσέειπε μέγας κορυθαίολος Ἕκτωρ·   440
"ἦ καὶ ἐμοὶ τάδε πάντα μέλει, γύναι· ἀλλὰ μάλ' αἰνῶς
αἰδέομαι Τρῶας καὶ Τρῳάδας ἑλκεσιπέπλους,
αἴ κε κακὸς ὣς νόσφιν ἀλυσκάζω πολέμοιο·
οὐδέ με θυμὸς ἄνωγεν, ἐπεὶ μάθον ἔμμεναι ἐσθλὸς
αἰεὶ καὶ πρώτοισι μετὰ Τρώεσσι μάχεσθαι,   445
ἀρνύμενος πατρός τε μέγα κλέος ἠδ' ἐμὸν αὐτοῦ.
εὖ γὰρ ἐγὼ τόδε οἶδα κατὰ φρένα καὶ κατὰ θυμόν·
ἔσσεται ἦμαρ, ὅτ' ἄν ποτ' ὀλώλῃ Ἴλιος ἱρὴ
καὶ Πρίαμος καὶ λαὸς ἐυμμελίω Πριάμοιο.
ἀλλ' οὔ μοι Τρώων τόσσον μέλει ἄλγος ὀπίσσω,   450
οὔτ' αὐτῆς Ἑκάβης οὔτε Πριάμοιο ἄνακτος
οὔτε κασιγνήτων, οἵ κεν πολέες τε καὶ ἐσθλοὶ
ἐν κονίῃσι πέσοιεν ὑπ' ἀνδράσι δυσμενέεσσιν,
ὅσσον σεῦ, ὅτε κέν τις Ἀχαιῶν χαλκοχιτώνων
δακρυόεσσαν ἄγηται, ἐλεύθερον ἦμαρ ἀπούρας.   455
καί κεν ἐν Ἄργει ἐοῦσα πρὸς ἄλλης ἱστὸν ὑφαίνοις,
καί κεν ὕδωρ φορέοις Μεσσηΐδος ἢ Ὑπερείης

433 στῆσον: 'position', 'station'.

434 Note the change of tense. The vulnerability of the wall is described in the following lines.

435 τῇ: 'at this point'.

437 Ἀτρεΐδας: plural, 'sons of Atreus', Agamemnon and Menelaos.

438 πού τίς: 'someone no doubt' (the accents are thrown back from σφιν).
θεοπροπίων: εἰδώς is often followed by gen., 'with a good knowledge of oracles'.

439 αὐτῶν: 'their own'.
ἀνώγει: present tense as if from ἀνώγω.

443 'if I were skulking about like a coward away from the war'.

444 ἔμμεναι: 'how to be'.
ἐσθλός: 'brave', the opposite of κακός in 443.

446 πατρός: 'for my father'.
αὐτοῦ: gets its case ending from the idea of possession inherent in ἐμόν, translate ἐμόν αὐτοῦ 'for myself', 'my own'. This line together with the previous four lines exemplifies the heroic pursuit of glory and the terrible shame incurred by being branded a coward.

447 τόδε: refers to what comes in the next two lines.

449 ἐυμμελίω: genitive singular.

450 ἄλγος: with genitives, 'sorrow for....'.

453 πέσοιεν: with κεν in a future sense, 'will fall'.

455 ἐλεύθερον ἦμαρ: 'freedom', see 463 for the opposite δούλιον ἦμαρ.

456 Ἄργει: here seems to mean Greece in general or possibly the Peloponnese.
ἐοῦσα: HF 19E.
πρὸς ἄλλης: 'at the orders of another woman'.

457 Μεσσηίδος ἢ Ὑπερείης: 'from the spring Messeis or Hypereia'. The spring of Hypereia, mentioned in Iliad II 734, is firmly sited in Thessaly. Messeis is more of a mystery. Pausanias places it at Therapne in Lakonia.

πόλλ' ἀεκαζομένη, κρατερὴ δ' ἐπικείσετ' ἀνάγκη·
καί ποτέ τις εἴπησιν ἰδὼν κατὰ δάκρυ χέουσαν·
'Ἕκτορος ἥδε γυνή, ὃς ἀριστεύεσκε μάχεσθαι   460
Τρώων ἱπποδάμων, ὅτε Ἴλιον ἀμφεμάχοντο.'
ὥς ποτέ τις ἐρέει, σοὶ δ' αὖ νέον ἔσσεται ἄλγος
χήτεϊ τοιοῦδ' ἀνδρός, ἀμύνειν δούλιον ἦμαρ.
ἀλλά με τεθνηῶτα χυτὴ κατὰ γαῖα καλύπτοι,
πρίν γέ τι σῆς τε βοῆς σοῦ θ' ἑλκηθμοῖο πυθέσθαι." 465

*Hektor kisses his son and prays Zeus to make him a
valiant warrior. He sends Andromache back to her
house.*

ὣς εἰπὼν οὗ παιδὸς ὀρέξατο φαίδιμος Ἕκτωρ·
ἂψ δ' ὁ πάις πρὸς κόλπον ἐϋζώνοιο τιθήνης
ἐκλίνθη ἰάχων, πατρὸς φίλου ὄψιν ἀτυχθείς,
ταρβήσας χαλκόν τε ἰδὲ λόφον ἱππιοχαίτην,
δεινὸν ἀπ' ἀκροτάτης κόρυθος νεύοντα νοήσας.   470
ἐκ δ' ἐγέλασσε πατήρ τε φίλος καὶ πότνια μήτηρ.
αὐτίκ' ἀπὸ κρατὸς κόρυθ' εἵλετο φαίδιμος Ἕκτωρ,
καὶ τὴν μὲν κατέθηκεν ἐπὶ χθονὶ παμφανόωσαν,
αὐτὰρ ὅ γ' ὃν φίλον υἱὸν ἐπεὶ κύσε πῆλέ τε χερσίν,
εἶπε δ' ἐπευξάμενος Διί τ' ἄλλοισίν τε θεοῖσιν·   475
"Ζεῦ ἄλλοι τε θεοί, δότε δὴ καὶ τόνδε γενέσθαι
παῖδ' ἐμόν, ὡς καὶ ἐγώ περ, ἀριπρεπέα Τρώεσσιν,
ὧδε βίην τ' ἀγαθὸν καὶ Ἰλίου ἶφι ἀνάσσειν·
καί ποτέ τις εἴποι 'πατρός γ' ὅδε πολλὸν ἀμείνων'
ἐκ πολέμου ἀνιόντα· φέροι δ' ἔναρα βροτόεντα   480

458 ἐπικείσετ(αι): supply 'you' as object.

459 εἴπῃσιν: subjunctive, HF 15, 'someone may say'.
     κατά ... χέουσαν: tmesis. Supply σέ with χέουσαν
     as object of ἰδών.

463 χήτεϊ: 'because of your lack of'.
     ἀμύνειν: after τοιοῦδε.
     δούλιον ἦμαρ: 'slavery', see note on 455.

464 κατά ... καλύπτοι: tmesis.

465 'before I have any knowledge of your cries as you
     are dragged off'.

466 οὖ: HF 9B.
     The following passage is justly famous for its deli-
     cate description and warm human touches. It pro-
     vides a welcome relief after the gloomy prophecy
     of Hektor (450-465) and yet because we all know
     that Hektor and Astyanax are soon to die and
     Andromache become a slave there is also an under-
     current of great sadness.

469 τε ἰδέ: for τε ... καί, 'both ... and'.
     This line explains ἀτυχθείς of 468.

470 δεινόν: with νεύοντα, 'nodding grimly'.

471 ἐκ ... ἐγέλασσε: 'laughed aloud'.

473 τήν: HF 20A, i.e. the helmet.

475 δ(έ): an example of the so-called apodotic δέ, cf.
     146 and note.

476 δότε: 'grant that'.

477 ἀριπρεπέα Τρώεσσιν: 'very distinguished among the
     Trojans'.

478 ὧδε: 'like me'.
     βίην τ' ἀγαθόν: 'notable for his strength', cf. βοὴν
     ἀγαθός (12).

480 ἀνιόντα: should be taken as object of εἴποι, 'may
     someone say of him returning from ...'.
     φέροι: the mood shows that this is also a wish.

κτείνας δήιον ἄνδρα, χαρείη δὲ φρένα μήτηρ."

ὣς εἰπὼν ἀλόχοιο φίλης ἐν χερσὶν ἔθηκεν
παῖδ' ἑόν· ἡ δ' ἄρα μιν κηώδεϊ δέξατο κόλπῳ
δακρυόεν γελάσασα· πόσις δ' ἐλέησε νοήσας,
χειρί τέ μιν κατέρεξεν, ἔπος τ' ἔφατ' ἔκ τ' ὀνόμαζεν·   485
"δαιμονίη, μή μοί τι λίην ἀκαχίζεο θυμῷ·
οὐ γάρ τίς μ' ὑπὲρ αἶσαν ἀνὴρ Ἄιδι προϊάψει·
μοῖραν δ' οὔ τινά φημι πεφυγμένον ἔμμεναι ἀνδρῶν,
οὐ κακόν, οὐδὲ μὲν ἐσθλόν, ἐπὴν τὰ πρῶτα γένηται.
ἀλλ' εἰς οἶκον ἰοῦσα τὰ σ' αὐτῆς ἔργα κόμιζε,   490
ἱστόν τ' ἠλακάτην τε, καὶ ἀμφιπόλοισι κέλευε
ἔργον ἐποίχεσθαι· πόλεμος δ' ἄνδρεσσι μελήσει
πᾶσιν, ἐμοὶ δὲ μάλιστα, τοὶ Ἰλίῳ ἐγγεγάασιν."

*Andromache and her women mourn for Hektor as one
already dead.*

ὣς ἄρα φωνήσας κόρυθ' εἵλετο φαίδιμος Ἕκτωρ
ἵππουριν· ἄλοχος δὲ φίλη οἶκόνδε βεβήκειν   495
ἐντροπαλιζομένη θαλερὸν κατὰ δάκρυ χέουσα.
αἶψα δ' ἔπειθ' ἵκανε δόμους εὖ ναιετάοντας
Ἕκτορος ἀνδροφόνοιο, κιχήσατο δ' ἔνδοθι πολλὰς
ἀμφιπόλους, τῇσιν δὲ γόον πάσῃσιν ἐνῶρσεν.
αἱ μὲν ἔτι ζωὸν γόον Ἕκτορα ᾧ ἐνὶ οἴκῳ·   500
οὐ γάρ μιν ἔτ' ἔφαντο ὑπότροπον ἐκ πολέμοιο
ἵξεσθαι προφυγόντα μένος καὶ χεῖρας Ἀχαιῶν.

481 φρένα: 'in her heart'.

483 ἑόν: HF 9B.

484 δακρυόεν γελάσασα: the juxtaposition of these two
words is highly emphatic especially as they come
at the beginning of a line and yet at the end of
their sentence, 'smiling through her tears'.
δακρυόεν, being neuter, is adverbial.

486 δαιμονίη: see note on 326.
μοι: 'on my account'.

487 ὑπὲρ αἶσαν: 'beyond what is fated', i.e. before
my time.

488 οὔ τινά ... πεφυγμένον ἔμμεναι ἀνδρῶν: 'no man
exists who has escaped', i.e. no one is free from
fate.

489 ἐπὴν ... γένηται: 'from the first moment that he
is born'.

490 τὰ σ' αὐτῆς: see note on 446.

491 Hektor outlines the traditional roles of men and
women in Homeric society.

493 τοί: for οἵ, HF 20C, refers back to πᾶσιν.

497 ἐὺ ναιετάοντας: see note on 370.

499 τῆσιν ... πάσησιν: HF 20A and HF 4D, 'in them all'.

500 γόον: 3rd pl. imperf. of γοάω, 'they lamented for'.

The meeting of Hektor and Andromache.

Paris overtakes Hektor and the two leave the town together.

οὐδὲ Πάρις δήθυνεν ἐν ὑψηλοῖσι δόμοισιν,

ἀλλ' ὅ γ' ἐπεὶ κατέδυ κλυτὰ τεύχεα ποικίλα χαλκῷ,

σεύατ' ἔπειτ' ἀνὰ ἄστυ, ποσὶ κραιπνοῖσι πεποιθώς.   505

ὡς δ' ὅτε τις στατὸς ἵππος, ἀκοστήσας ἐπὶ φάτνῃ,

δεσμὸν ἀπορρήξας θείῃ πεδίοιο κροαίνων,

εἰωθὼς λούεσθαι ἐϋρρεῖος ποταμοῖο,

κυδιόων· ὑψοῦ δὲ κάρη ἔχει, ἀμφὶ δὲ χαῖται

ὤμοις ἀΐσσονται· ὁ δ' ἀγλαΐηφι πεποιθώς,   510

ῥίμφα ἑ γοῦνα φέρει μετά τ' ἤθεα καὶ νομὸν ἵππων·

ὣς υἱὸς Πριάμοιο Πάρις κατὰ Περγάμου ἄκρης,

τεύχεσι παμφαίνων ὥς τ' ἠλέκτωρ, ἐβεβήκειν

καγχαλόων, ταχέες δὲ πόδες φέρον. αἶψα δ' ἔπειτα

Ἕκτορα δῖον ἔτετμεν ἀδελφεόν, εὖτ' ἄρ' ἔμελλεν   515

στρέψεσθ' ἐκ χώρης, ὅθι ᾗ ὀάριζε γυναικί.

τὸν πρότερος προσέειπεν Ἀλέξανδρος θεοειδής·

"ἠθεῖ', ἦ μάλα δή σε καὶ ἐσσύμενον κατερύκω

δηθύνων, οὐδ' ἦλθον ἐναίσιμον, ὡς ἐκέλευες;"

   τὸν δ' ἀπαμειβόμενος προσέφη κορυθαίολος Ἕκτωρ·   520

"δαιμόνι', οὐκ ἄν τίς τοι ἀνήρ, ὃς ἐναίσιμος εἴη,

ἔργον ἀτιμήσειε μάχης, ἐπεὶ ἄλκιμός ἐσσι·

ἀλλὰ ἑκὼν μεθιεῖς τε καὶ οὐκ ἐθέλεις· τὸ δ' ἐμὸν κῆρ

ἄχνυται ἐν θυμῷ, ὅθ' ὑπὲρ σέθεν αἴσχε' ἀκούω

πρὸς Τρώων, οἳ ἔχουσι πολὺν πόνον εἵνεκα σεῖο.   525

ἀλλ' ἴομεν· τὰ δ' ὄπισθεν ἀρεσσόμεθ', αἴ κέ ποθι Ζεὺς

503   The end of the book relieves the tension by directing our attention to the wayward Paris.

504   κατέδυ: HF 12B.
ποικίλα χαλκῷ: 'skilfully wrought in bronze'.

505   ποσί ... πεποιθώς: 'confident in the speed of his feet'.

506-511   This vivid simile emphasises the sudden release of pent-up strength in a stallion conscious of its beauty and speed. Paris, a proud and vain man, has been confined in Troy since the end of Book 3, and now goes striding quickly down to the plain. The gallop of the horse mirrors Paris' eager descent; the χαῖται of the stallion remind us of the horse-hair plume on Paris' helmet. Paris, however, was not, unlike the stallion, going in search of ladies! Vergil reworked this simile (Aen. XI 492ff.) as Turnus descends to do battle with Aeneas.

507   πεδίοιο: for this genitive see note on 2.

508   ἐυρρεῖος ποταμοῖο: partitive gen., 'in the waters of a fine-flowing river'.

510   ἀγλαΐηφι: HF 4E, the ending acts as a dative here.
πεποιθώς: highlights the similarity between the horse and Paris, see 505.

510-11   The subject ὁ δέ becomes the object ἑ. This is called 'anacoluthon'.

511   φέρει μετά: 'take him in search of'.
ἵππων: feminine.

515   ἔτετμεν: HF 12B.

518   ἠθεῖ(ε): 'brother'. In this and the following line Paris shows by his self-justifying tone that Hektor does not approve of him and his behaviour.

521   δαιμόνι(ε): see note on 326. Here 'my dear brother'.

522   ἔργον ... μάχης: '(would scorn) your achievements in battle'.

523   τό: for τοῦτο, HF 20B. It is the object of ἄχνυται, 'is grieved at this', and is explained by ὅθ' ... 'when...' in 524.

524   σέθεν: HF 9A.

526   ἴομεν: subjunctive, HF 15, 'let us go'.
τά: HF 20B. Hektor is referring to their quarrel.

δώῃ ἐπουρανίοισι θεοῖς αἰειγενέτῃσιν

κρητῆρα στήσασθαι ἐλεύθερον ἐν μεγάροισιν,

ἐκ Τροίης ἐλάσαντας ἐυκνήμιδας Ἀχαιούς."

The arming of Hektor; from an early red-
figure amphora by Euthymides, now in Munich.

527 δώη: supply ἡμᾶς, 'grants us to'.
ϑεοῖς: 'in honour of the gods'.

528 κρητῆρα ... ἐλεύϑερον: 'a mixing bowl to celebrate
our freedom'.

529 ἐλάσαντας: aor. part. of ἐλαύνω. We would expect
dative to agree with ἡμῖν supplied after δώη ('grant
to us') but in such cases it is not uncommon for the
strict agreement to be broken and a sort of acc. +
inf. introduced: 'if Zeus grants (to) us having
driven the Greeks ... to set up a mixing bowl ...
to the gods'.

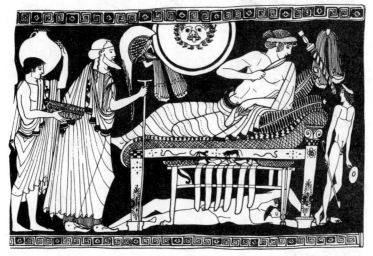

Ransom of Hektor; from a cup (*skyphos*) by the Brygos
Painter; Kunsthistorisches Museum, Vienna.

Iliupersis (Sack of Troy), showing from left to right
Aeneas with Anchises and Ascanius, Ajax seizing Cassandra,
Neoptolomos attacking Priam who had dead Astyanax on his
knees, Andromache (?) facing Greek warrior; from a water
jug (*kalpis*) by the Kleophrades painter, ca. 490 B.C.;
Museo Nazionale 2422, Naples.

APPENDIX 1

SOME BASIC HOMERIC FORMS

Note: corresponding Attic forms are given in brackets. The
line references are from Book 6.

1 *Vowels*

(a)   η for Attic long α:

e.g.   οἵη (οἵα) ˙146
λίην (λίαν) 100

(b)   ου sometimes for o:

e.g.   δουρί (δόρατι) 32
κούρη (κόρη) 304

2 *Consonants*

(a)   doubling:

e.g.   ὀπίσσω (ὀπίσω) 357
μέσση (μέση) 181
ὅττι (ὅτι) 177

(b)   change of position:

e.g.   κραδίη (καρδία)
κάρτιστον (κράτιστον) 98

(c)   assimilation with loss of final vowel - often
with ἀνά and κατά:

e.g.   κάκτανε (κατάκτανε) 164
κὰπ πεδίον (κατὰ πεδίον) 201
ἂμ πεδίον (ἀνὰ πεδίον) 71
κάλλιπε (κατέλιπε) 223

3 *The Digamma*

An old consonant (written 'F' in early inscriptions
and pronounced 'W'). Its original presence in certain words often affects scansion (see Appendix 4).
The following list gives some words which used to
begin with digamma:

65

ἄναξ   ἔργον
ἄστυ   ἐρέω
ἔαρ   ἔτος
εἶδος   Ἴλιον
εἴκοσι   ἶσος
ἑκάς   ἶφι
ἕκαστος   οἱ (dat.)
ἔλπω   οἴκαδε
ἔοικε   οἶκος
ἔπος   οἶνος

also ἰδ- stems from (ὁράω) (cf. Latin *vid-*)
and εἰπ- stems from λέγω

NOUNS

4   *First Declension*

(a)   masculine singular: a few nominatives in -α
        (names for Zeus):

          e.g.   μητίετα 198, νεφεληγερέτα

(b)   genitive singular: -αο, -εω (-ου)

          e.g.   ἐυρρείταο (ἐυρρείτου) 34, Πηληιάδεω

(c)   genitive plural: -αων, -εων (-ῶν):

          e.g.   ῥοάων 4, πυλάων 80, θεάων 305,
              ναυτέων

(d)   dative plural: -ῃσι, -ῃς (-αις):

          e.g.   κονίῃσιν 43, τῇσιν 499, πολλῇσι 241

(e)   old instrumental case: -φι(ν):

          e.g.   ἶφι 478, ἀγλαΐηφι 510

5   *Second Declension*

(a)   genitive singular: -οιο, -οο (-ου)

          e.g.   πεδίοιο 2, βιότοιο 14, ἀδελφεόο 61

(b)   dative plural: -οισι(ν) (οις)

          e.g.   ἑτάροισιν 6, Δαναοῖσι 84

6   *Third Declension*

(a)   doubling of σ in dative and sometimes also
doubling of the preceeding vowel:

e.g.   ποσσί (ποσί) 228
ἐπέεσσι (ἔπεσι) 325

(b)   uncontracted endings:

e.g.   ἔγχεα (ἔγχη) 226
ἀληθέος (ἀληθοῦς)

(c)   un-Attic forms also to be watched for with
nouns such as the following:

ἀνήρ   πατήρ
βασιλεύς   πόλις
κάρη   πολύς
νηῦς (ναῦς)

ADJECTIVES/ADVERBS

7   *Comparatives and Superlatives*

(κέρδος)	κέρδιον 410 (more profitable)	κερδιστος 153
ἄγχι (near)	ἄσσον 143	ἄγχιστα
(ἀρετή)	ἀρείων (better, braver)	ἄριστος 76

8   *Numerals*

(a)   feminine of 'one': ἴα, ἴαν, ἰῆς, ἰῇ as well
as μία etc. See ἰῷ 422 (dat. neuter).

(b)   'four' is πίσυρες as well as τέσσαρες.

PRONOUNS

9   (a)   personal:

first person: genitive singular: ἐμεῖο, ἐμεῦ,
μευ (ἐμοῦ/μου)
nominative plural: ἄμμες (ἡμεῖς)
accusative plural: ἄμμε (ἡμᾶς)
dative plural: ἄμμι(ν) (ἡμῖν)

second person: genitive singular: σεῖο, σέο, σεῦ
τεοῖο (σοῦ)

dative singular: τοι (σοι)
nominative plural: ὕμμες (ὑμεῖς)
accusative plural: ὕμμε (ὑμᾶς)
dative plural: ὕμμι(ν) (ὑμῖν)

third person: accusative singular: ἕε, ἕ, μιν
(αὐτόν -ήν -ό)
genitive singular: εἷο, ἕο, εὗ
(αὐτοῦ -ῆς)
dative singular: ἑοῖ, οἷ (αὐτῷ,
-ῇ)
accusative plural: σφέας, σφας,
σφε (αὐτούς, -άς)
genitive plural: σφείων, σφέων
(αὐτῶν)
dative plural: σφίσι, σφι(ν)
(αὐτοῖς - αἷς)

Note: genitive singular forms ἑμέθεν, σέθεν and ἕθεν
are also found.

(b) possessive:

ἁμός (ἡμέτερος)
τεός (σός)
ὑμός (ὑμέτερος)
ἑός, ὅς (for Latin *suus* - ἑαυτοῦ - 'his/her/
its own')
σφέτερος, σφός ('their own')

(c) interrogative (τίς):

genitive singular: τέο, τεῦ (τίνος)
dative singular: τέῳ, τῷ (τίνι)
genitive plural: τέων (τίνων)

(d) relative:

ἅσσα (ἅτινα/ἅττα - neuter plural of ὅστις)

VERBS

10 *Augment*

(a) augment is retained or omitted to suit the metre.

(b) consonants (λ, μ, ν, ρ) are sometimes doubled:

e.g. ἑλλίσσετο 45, ἕρριπτον

11   *Present and Imperfect*

(a)   differing forms of Present with the same meaning:

ἵκω, ἱκάνω, ἱκνέομαι (I come, go)
ἔδω, ἔσθω, ἐσθίω (I eat)

(b)   σ lost in 2nd person singular endings of
medio-passive verbs:

e.g. ἔρχεαι (ἔρχεσαι), κήδεαι 55

12   *Aorist*

(a)   frequent weak aorist endings in -σσα:

e.g. ἐγέλασσε 471, ἐκάλεσσα

(b)   unusual strong aorists to be noted:

φάν 108, from φημί (they said)
κέκλετο 287, from κέλομαι (she ordered)
τέτμεν 374, (no present) (he found)
κατέδυ 504, from καταδύω (he put on)
ἄλτο from ἄλλομαι (he swooped)

(c)   -εν (for Attic -ησαν) frequent in 3rd person
plural aorist passive:

e.g. ἐλέλιχθεν 109, from ἐλελίζω
ἔτραφεν from τρέφω

13   *Frequentative Forms*

The suffix -σκ denotes repeated action:

e.g. φιλέ-εσκεν 15, from φιλέω
καλέ-εσκε 402, from καλέω
ἀριστεύ-εσκε 460, from ἀριστεύω
ἔσκεν 19, from εἰμί (he used to be)

14   *Perfect and Pluperfect*

(a)   unusual forms to be noted:

ἐγγεγάασι 493, from ἐγγίγνομαι
βέβαμεν, βεβάασι from βαίνω
τέτλαθι, τετληώς from τλάω
ἴδμεν, ἴδμεναι from οἶδα

(b)   -αται and -ατο used for 3rd person plural
        middle and passive (Attic -νται, -ντο):

        e.g. τετράφαται from τρέπω (have
              been turned)
              ἔρχαται from εἴργω (have been
              enclosed)
              ἧατο from ἧμαι (sat)
              κείατο from κεῖμαι (ἔκειντο - they lay)

15   *Subjunctive*

        Active   Middle

        -ω   -ομαι
        -ῃς or -ῃσθα   -ηαι or εαι
        -ῃ or ῃσι   -εται
        -ομεν   -όμεθα
        -ετε   -ησθε
        -ωσι   -ωνται

16   *Optative*

        -ατο used for 3rd person plural middle (Attic -ντο):

        e.g. ἐξαπολοίατο 60, ἐποίατο

17   *Infinitive*

        Endings in -μεναι: δαήμεναι 150, μιγήμεναι 161
                   -έμεναι, -έμεν, -ειν: εἰπέμεναι, εἰπέμεν,
                   εἰπεῖν

18   *Contracted Verbs*

        (a)   verbs in -άω: assimilation is common

                e.g. ἀντιόωσιν (ἀντιάω) 127
                      γοόωσα (γοάω) 373

        (b)   verbs in -έω: usually left uncontracted but
                when contracted ε-ο and ε-ου become -ευ:

                e.g. καλεῦντες (καλέοντες/καλοῦντες)

                similar is ἔρχευ 280 contracted from ἔρχεο
                (Attic ἔρχου)

(c) verbs in -όω: usually contracted but
such forms as ἀρόωσι (ἀρόω), δηιόωντες
(δηιόω) occur.

19   *Verb 'to be'*

(a) present:

εἰμί
ἐσσί or εἰς
ἐστί
εἰμέν
ἐστέ
εἰσί or ἔασι

(b) imperfect:

ἔα or ἦα or ἔον
ἔησθα or ἦσθα
ἦεν or ἦν or ἔην or ἤην
ἦμεν
ἦτε
ἔσαν or ἦσαν

(c) subjunctive:

ἔω
ἔῃς
ἔῃσι or ἔῃ (3rd plural ἔωσι)

(d) infinitive:

ἔμμεναι or ἔμεναι or ἔμεν or ἔμμεν
or εἶναι

(e) participle:

ἐών, ἐοῦσα, ἐόν

DEFINITE ARTICLE

20   *The Attic Definite Article* (ὁ, ἡ, τό)

This has three uses in Homer:

(a) as personal pronoun (for αὐτόν, -ήν, -ό etc.)
(b) as demonstrative pronoun (for οὗτος, αὕτη,
       τοῦτο etc.)
(c) as a relative pronoun (for ὅς, ἥ, ὅ etc.)

The Trojan Horse, from the neck panel of a relief jar
(*pithos*) from Mykonos, seventh century B.C.

APPENDIX 2

'PREPOSITIONAL' USAGES

Words which in Attic Greek are prepositions governing
nouns or pronouns may be used in somewhat different
ways in Homer.   There are four main usages of such
words.

(a)   They may have exactly the same function as in
       Attic, although their meaning may be different
       in some cases (see vocabulary).

(b)   Their meaning may be the same as in (a), but
       they can follow the word which they are governing
       (properly called 'post-position'), e.g. lines 15
       and 39.   When prepositions of two syllables,
       which normally have an accent on the second syl-
       lable, are used in this way, the accent is trans-
       ferred to the first syllable.

(c)   In Homer's Greek the formation of a compound verb
       by attaching a preposition to a simple verb had
       not become an invariable process.   In many cases
       this *is* done, but in others the preposition can
       appear as a separate word, divided by other words
       from the verb to which it is attached in sense.
       This separation of the two parts of the compound
       is called 'tmesis', from the Greek verb τέμνω, 'I
       cut'.   Strictly speaking, this is a misnomer.   It
       is not that the preposition has been 'cut off' from
       the verb, but rather that its position with the
       verb has not yet become fixed.   E.g. πάρ ... ἔστη
       43, ἐπί ... θῆκε 357 and many others.

(d)   These words may also appear on their own, neither
       governing a noun or pronoun, nor in 'tmesis'.   In
       these cases they can be thought of as 'adverbial'.
       Often the best way of translating the word is by
       supplying a pronoun such as 'it' which the pre-
       position can then govern (e.g. line 117).

FORMULAE

As is stated in the Introduction, scholars have begun
to show us how the Homeric poems belong to an 'oral'
tradition. The idea of oral poetry is quite foreign
to our experience and it is difficult for us to understand how the bards 'composed' poems on the spur of
the moment as they sat before their audience. They
had no written text (for the art of writing had been
lost in Greece for several centuries) and they did not
learn their lines off by heart. Each telling of the
story used the same basic facts but the wording varied
on each occasion. Scholars cannot fully explain how
this was done, since it is impossible to understand
completely an age which has left no written records.
However, research has been done recently into oral
traditions which have survived into the 20th century.
There is still no agreement on the details and further
work is producing new ideas. All agree, however, that
one feature of the oral tradition which is of paramount
importance is the use of 'formulae'.

Formulae can be loosely defined as stock lines or
phrases whose use can show us something of the oral
poet's art.

Whole lines can be repeated word for word on different
occasions. Sometimes these are 'repeats' of lines used
only in this book. (See lines 93-97, repeated 274-278).
Sometimes, however, there are lines which occur not
only in one book but throughout the *Iliad*. Such lines
often describe things which recur regularly, such as
the fall of darkness or the coming of dawn, e.g.:

Dusk - ἦμος δ' ἥέλιος κατέδυ καὶ ἐπὶ κνέφας ἦλθεν
Dawn - ἦμος δ' ἠριγένεια φάνη ῥοδοδάκτυλος Ἠώς

In giving a reply made by someone, there may be slight
variations to suit the context (see lines 263, 440).
This shows that the formulaic method of composition could
still be flexible, since any part of the line can be
changed by substituting other words of the same metrical
pattern.

For this reason phrases of a particular pattern commonly
occur at the same place in the line. For example, a
preposition plus a noun giving the metrical pattern
'short-short/long-short' in the 4th and 5th feet (see

Appendix 4) is found in many places, e.g. line 52 ἐπὶ
νῆας or line 50 ἐπὶ νηυσίν. This is only one example
of a series of such patterns for use in various parts
of the line. This example gives us a glimpse of the
kind of material, already partly fixed, which the bard
had in his head as he recited the poems. He used this
material in many different ways in different places in
order to produce the varied patterns which we have in
the poems.

One example of formulaic phrases which strikes readers
of Homer is the use of a stock adjective plus a noun,
frequently a proper noun, e.g. βοὴν ἀγαθὸς Διομήδης 12;
κρείων ᾿Αγαμέμνων 63; κορυθαίολος ῞Εκτωρ 116; δῖος
᾿Αχιλλεύς 423; ἐυκνήμιδας ᾿Αχαιούς 529. This very obvious feature of Homer's style first drew attention to
what is now spoken of as 'formulaic'. Often these
'stock epithets' are meaningful in their context and add
to the description, but sometimes they are purely traditional. This occurs most frequently with proper names
but may also be seen in other cases. In Line 332 it
does not seem very meaningful to refer to Paris as
θεοειδής when he is sulking at home away from the battle.

It must not be thought that the oral poet made up his
poetry simply by arranging in different orders a stock
of ready-made phrases. There are many formulaic phrases,
but the greater part of the story was told in lines not
repeated elsewhere. However, the usefulness of formulae is obvious. A poet called upon to recite at short
notice would inevitably make these an integral part of
his poem. Homer uses them so skilfully that his poetry
in its written form still reads naturally and presents a
vivid narrative.

Rhapsode; from wine-
jar (amphora) by the
Kleophrades Painter,
ca. 480 B.C.; British
Museum, London.

APPENDIX 4

METRE AND SCANSION

In reading and appreciating poetry, one of the most
important aspects is the structure of the verse, or the
'rules' according to which the poet composed each line.
In English poetry the structure is based on 'accent'
or 'stress' and this is sometimes accompanied by
rhyme. Greek poets did not use either of these techniques. For them the important factor was the 'length'
of each syllable in a word. Long and short syllables
were arranged in a pattern which could be varied within certain limits.

The name given to each of Homer's lines is 'hexameter'
because it is composed of six parts which we call 'feet'.
Each foot (μέτρον) can consist of a long syllable and
two short syllables (which we mark -ᴗᴗ) or two long
syllables (--), except the sixth foot which can be
either -- or -ᴗ. We can write this metrical pattern
in the following way:

$$-\underline{ᴗ}\underline{ᴗ}/-\underline{ᴗ}\underline{ᴗ}/-\underline{ᴗ}\underline{ᴗ}/-\underline{ᴗ}\underline{ᴗ}/-\underline{ᴗ}\underline{ᴗ}/-\underline{ᴗ}$$

A foot marked -ᴗᴗ is called a 'dactyl' and one marked
-- a 'spondee'. The process of marking the syllables
and feet in a line is called 'scansion'.

As can be seen from the pattern above, a line can consist of between 12 and 17 syllables. This gives flex-
ibility within certain limits.

In such a long line it is natural that there should be
places where breaks between words give a chance to take
breath. The name given to such a break in the middle
of a foot is 'caesura' (from the Latin word *caedo*, I
cut). The commonest or 'weak' caesura (indicated by //)
occurs between the two short syllables of a third foot
dactyl:

4: μεσσηγὺς Σιμό / εντος // ίδ / ὲ Ξάνθοιο ῥοάων
7: ἄνδρα βαλὼν ὅς ἄρ / ιστος // ἐν / ὶ Θρήκεσσι
   τέτυκτο

Almost as frequent is the 'strong' caesura after the
first syllable of the third foot:

1: Τρώων δ' οἰώ / θη // καὶ 'Αχ / αιῶν φύλοπις αἰνή

77

11: αἰχμὴ χαλκεῖ / η // τὸν / δὲ σκότος ὄσσε κάλυψεν

Occasionally there is no break in the third foot and
the caesura comes after the first syllable of the fourth
foot:

3: ἀλλήλων ἰθυνομέν / ων // χαλκ / ήρεα δοῦρα

A break at the end of a foot is called a 'diaeresis'
(from the Greek word meaning 'separation'). A favour-
ite diaeresis is after the fourth foot. This is called
the 'Bucolic Diaeresis' because it was frequently em-
ployed by writers of Bucolic (i.e. pastoral) poetry.
When there is a Bucolic Diaeresis, the fourth foot is
almost always a dactyl:

5: Αἴας δὲ πρῶτος Τελαμ / ώνιος // ἕρκος 'Αχαιῶν
16: ἀλλά οἱ οὔ τις τῶν γε τότ' / ἤρκεσε // λυγρὸν
    ὄλεθρον

Digamma

This consonant (written 'F'.and pronounced 'W') was
used in early Greek but had disappeared from Homer's
dialect. It is not written in Homeric texts. In com-
posing his lines, Homer sometimes takes account of the
digamma but at other times he ignores it. (In line
459 it is observed before Fεῖπῃσιν but ignored before
Fἰδών). The effects of the digamma will be mentioned
in the paragraphs which follow. For a list of some of
the words which had initial digamma see Appendix 1,
paragraph 3.

Length of Vowels

ε and ο are short. α, ι, υ are sometimes long by nature
(e.g. θεᾱ, κληῑδι, ἐδῡτην), sometimes short (e.g. πολλᾰ,
φυλοπῐς, κορῠθος). η and ω and all diphthongs are long.

Length of Syllables

A short syllable is one which contains a short vowel followed by another vowel (e.g. χαλκηρἔα), or by a single
consonant (e.g. ἄνδρᾰ βαλών).

A long syllable is one which contains a long vowel or
a diphthong (e.g. Τρῶῶν, ὀῑωῶθη, μαχῆ, αἰχμῆ, Διομῆδῆς.)

A long syllable is also produced when a short vowel
is followed by either a double consonant (ζ, ξ, ψ)
or two or more single consonants, one of which may be
the unwritten digamma (e.g. ἰδὲ Ξάνθοιο, κόρυθὸς φάλον,
ἔβαλε πρῶτος, αὐτὰρ Ϝοἱ).

Notes

1   A short vowel before πρ, τρ, πλ and
     some other combinations is optional
     (e.g. δὲ πρῶτος 5, but Ἱππολόχοιὸ
     προσηύδα 144).

2   A short vowel is sometimes lengthened
     before one consonant only (usually δ,
     λ, μ, ν, σ) or where internal digamma
     has dropped out. This often occurs
     also before a pause in the sense (e.g.
     κατὰ λαπάρην 64, ποτὶ μέγαρ' 286, πρὶν
     αὖτ' 81, πόλις 'Εφύρη 152, ἔδεισεν for
     ἔδϜεισεν).

3   In such examples as θυμὸν ἑκάστου 72,
     τἶέν ἄναξ 173, ἔνθ' ἐσᾶν οἱ, μέγᾶν
     'Ιλίου and many others the digamma is
     ignored and the vowel left short.

Hiatus

This occurs where a vowel at the end of a word is left
unaffected by a vowel at the beginning of the next word:
ῥυμῷ αὐτώ 40, ζώγρει 'Ατρέος 46, κασιγνήτῳ ἀπίθησεν 102,
ἢ εἰνατέρων 378 and many others. Hiatus is avoided in
two ways:

(1)   *Elision*

      A short vowel is 'elided' (i.e. cut off) before
      an initial vowel (e.g. τεύχε(α) ἐσύλα 28, ἔλ(ε)
      ἵππω 38, ἄξαντ(ε) ἐν 40 and many more.

      Notes

      1   The verbal ending -αι in certain forms
           may be elided (e.g. βούλομ(αι), λίσσομ
           (αι)). There are no examples in Book 6
           but see *Iliad* I, 117, 168, 283.

      2   Digamma, when observed, prevents elision;
           when ignored, allows it: μελιηδέα Ϝοῖνον
           258, digamma observed; ἐθέλησ' Ϝειπόντος,

digamma ignored.

(2)   *Correption*

A long vowel or diphthong in hiatus may be scanned
as short. This is very common (e.g. ὀζῷ ἔνι 39,
δέξαι ἄποινα 46 etc.).

Correption should not not occur before initial
digamma, but in παμποικιλοῖ Fέργα 289 the digamma
has been ignored.

The unwritten digamma obviates many apparent
examples of hiatus (e.g. προτὶ F"Ιλιον, φύει Fέαρος
148 and many others).

When elision and correption have been applied
and allowance made for digamma, there are still
very many examples of true hiatus in Homer. These
often occur at the caesura (e.g. 'Ευσσώρου 'Ακάμαντ'
8), at the stress at the beginning of a foot (e.g.
ἐυκτιμένῃ ἐν 'Αρίσβῃ 13), or after ἤ (e.g. ἤ εἰνατέρων 378, ἤ ἐς 379).

Synizesis

This occurs when two vowels (not forming a diphthong) in
the same word or in successive words are run together and
pronounced as one long syllable (e.g. δηῖοῖσι 82, χρυσέος
320).

Practice

Some lines from Book 6 are scanned below according to the
scheme outlined in this Appendix. These rules will enable
you to cope with the great majority of lines in Homer.
For further information, see 'Greek Metre' by D.S. Raven
(Faber, 1962). It should, however, be remembered that
the best way to appreciate Homer's metre is to listen to
it. If someone familiar with Homer reads some lines, it
should then be possible for the beginner to practise for
himself, hearing the music of Homer far better than by
reliance on a set of rules.

```
    _    _  /    _ /    ˘  ˘/_    ˘ /˘/_ _/_   ˘  ˘/_  ˘
56  ἀνδρῶν ἤ σοι ἄριστα πεποίηται κατὰ οἶκον
```

(weak caesura; correption σοι ἄριστα; apparent hiatus
κατὰ Fοῖκον).

81 — ⌣ ⌣/— ⌣ ⌣/— // — / — — / — ⌣ ⌣/— —
πάντῃ ἐποιχόμενοι πρίν αὖτ' ἐν χερσί γυναικῶν

(strong caesura; correption πάντῃ ἐποιχόμενοι;
πρίν lengthened at caesura).

210 — ⌣ ⌣/— ⌣ ⌣/— ⌣// ⌣ /— ⌣ ⌣/— —/— —
ἔν τ' 'Εφύρῃ ἐγένοντο καί ἐν Λυκίῃ εὑρείῃ

(weak caesura: real hiatus 'Εφύρῃ ἐγένοντο
and Λυκίῃ εὑρείῃ; correption καί ἐν; spondee
in 5th foot).

272 — ⌣ ⌣/— ⌣ ⌣/—// —/ — ⌣ ⌣/// — ⌣ ⌣ / — —
ἔστιν ἐνί μεγάρῳ καί τοι πολύ φίλτατος αὐτῇ

(strong caesura; ἐνι lengthened before μ;
Bucolic Diaeresis).

287 — ⌣ ⌣/ — ⌣ ⌣/— —/ — // ⌣ ⌣// — ⌣ ⌣ / — —
κέκλετο ταί δ' ἄρ' ἀόλλισσαν κατά ἄστυ γεραιάς

(caesura in 4th foot; apparent hiatus κατά ἄστυ;
Bucolic Diaeresis).

306 — — / — —/ — // ⌣⌣/— ⌣⌣ //— ⌣ ⌣/ — ⌣
ἄξον δή ἔγχος Διομήδεος ἠδέ καί αὐτον

(strong caesura; real hiatus δή ἔγχος; correption
καί αὐτόν; Bucolic Diaeresis).

Zeus; from exterior of
wine-cup (kylix) by the
painter Oltos, ca. 515 B.C.;
Museo Nazionale RC6848,
Tarquinia.

VOCABULARY

Difficult verbs forms are listed but parts of common Attic irregular verbs and Homeric forms referred to in the Notes are not included.

The following abbreviations are used throughout the vocabulary:

acc.	accusative	*m.*	masculine
act.	active	*mid.*	middle
adj.	adjective	*n.*	neuter
adv.	adverb	*nom.*	nominative
aor.	aorist	*opt.*	optative
conj.	conjunction	*part.*	participle
dat.	dative	*pass.*	passive
f.	feminine	*perf.*	perfect
fut.	future	*pl.*	plural
gen.	genitive	*pluperf.*	pluperfect
imperf.	imperfect	*pres.*	present
indic.	indicative	*pron.*	pronoun
inf.	infinitive	*rel.*	relative
intrans.	intransitive	*sing.*	singular
1.	line (*see on* 1.	*subj.*	subjunctive
	refers to	*trans.*	transitive
	notes)	*voc.*	vocative

A

ἀγαθός, ή, όν noble; good (at); valiant.

ἀγακλυτός, όν renowned, famous.

ἀγαπητός, ή, όν beloved.

ἀγαυός, ή, όν noble.

ἄγε (*exclamation*) come!

ἀγελείη *f. adj.* driver of the spoil (of Athene).

ἀγκύλος, ον curved.

ἀγλαΐη, ης *f.* splendour, beauty.

ἄγνυμι break.

ἄγριος, ον savage, fierce.

ἄγυια, ῆς *f.* street.

ἄγχι *adv.* nearby,

ἄγω, *aor.* ἤγαγον bring; lead away.

ἀδελφεός, οῦ *m.* brother.

ἀείρω bring out, fetch; lift up.

ἀεκαζόμενος, η, ον unwilling, resisting.

ἀέξω increase.

ἄζομαι fear (to), shrink from.

ἀθάνατος, ον immortal; (*as a noun*) god.

αἰ *same as* εἰ

αἰγίοχος, ον aegisbearing.

αἰδέομαι feel shame before.

αἰδοῖος, η, ον chaste;
modest.
αἰεί, αἰέν adv. always.
αἰειγενέτης, ου everlast-
ing.
αἴθομαι burn, blaze.
αἴθουσα, ης f. colonnade.
αἴθοψ, οπος sparkling.
αἷμα, ατος n. blood.
αἰνός, ή, όν terrible,
frightful.
αἰνῶς adv. very much,
exceedingly.
αἰπεινός, ή, όν steep.
αἰπύς, εῖα, ύ utter;
steep.
αἱρέω seize, capture,
take off.
αἶσα fate (see on Il. 333,
487).
αἴσιμα adv. rightly,
properly.
ἀίσσω and mid. leap;
toss.
αἶσχος, εος n. reproach.
αἰσχρός, όν abusive;
shameful.
αἰσχύνω disgrace.
αἰτέω ask.
αἰχμή, ῆς f. point,
spear-point.
αἰχμήτης, ου m. spearman,
warrior.
αἶψα adv. soon.
ἀκαχίζομαι grieve.
ἀκήδεστος, ον uncared for.
ἄκοιτις, ιος f. wife.
ἀκοστήσας adj. well-fed.
ἀκούω hear, listen to
(with gen.).
ἄκρος, η, ον top of.
ἀλάομαι wander.
ἄλγος, εος n. sorrow,
grief.
ἀλεείνω avoid, shrink
from.
ἀλέξω ' (+ dat.) help.
ἀλέομαι avoid
ἀληθής, ές true
ἀλίγκιος, ον like (to).
ἀλκή, ῆς f. prowess;
strength.

ἄλκιμος, ον brave;
stalwart.
ἀλλά conj. but.
ἀλλήλων (no nom.) one
another.
ἄλλομαι leap.
ἄλλος, η, ο other.
ἄλοχος, ου f. wife.
ἅλς, ἁλός f. sea.
ἆλτο 3rd sing. 2nd aor. of
ἅλλομαι
ἀλυσκάζω skulk; shrink.
ἄμ for ἀνά (+ acc.) along
throughout.
ἅμα adv. together; at
the same time.
ἅμα prep. (+ dat.) along
with.
ἀμαιμάκετος, η, ον raging.
ἀμβατός, ον easily scaled.
ἀμείβομαι answer.
ἀμείβω (+ acc. and gen.)
exchange (x) for (y).
ἀμείνων, ον better; more
valiant.
ἄμμορος, ον hapless.
ἀμός for ἐμός my.
ἀμύμων, ονος excellent,
blameless.
ἀμύνω ward off, defend,
help (+ dat.).
ἀμφί adv. around (him).
ἀμφί (+ acc.) around.
ἀμφιβαίνω surround, en-
compass.
ἀμφιδαίω blaze around.
ἀμφιδέδηε 3rd sing. perf. of
ἀμφιδαίω.
ἀμφικύπελλος, ον with two
handles.
ἀμφιμάχομαι fight around.
ἀμφίπολος, ου m. and f.
servant.
ἀμφότεροι both sides.
ἄμφω both.
ἄν particle same as κε(ν).
ἄνα adv. for imperative up!
ἀνά (+ acc.) through.
ἀναγκαίη, ης f. necessity.
ἀνάγκη, ης f. necessity.
ἀνάγω bring by sea.
ἀνάλκεια, ης f. (also in pl.)

lack of spirit.
ἀνανεύω deny, refuse a
prayer.
ἄναξ, ἄνακτος m. lord,
king.
ἀνάσσω rule over (+ gen. or
dat.).
ἀνασχεῖν aor. inf. act. of
ἀνέχω.
ἀνατρέπω turn over; (mid.)
fall over.
ἀνδροφόνος, ον man-slaying,
murderous.
ἄνειμι return.
ἄνεμος, ου m. wind.
ἀνέρχομαι come back.
ἀνετράπετο 3rd sing. aor.
mid. of ἀνατρέπω.
ἀνέχω, aor. ἀνέσχον hold
up, raise.
ἀνῆκεν 3rd sing. aor. of
ἀνίημι.
ἀνήρ, ἀνδρός or ἀνέρος m.
man; warrior.
ἄνθρωπος, ου m. man;
(in pl.) mankind, people.
ἀνίημι send back.
ἄνιπτος, ον unwashed.
ἀντάω (+ dat.) come to
meet.
ἀντιάνειρα f. adj. a match
for men.
ἀντιάω (+ dat.) meet;
oppose.
ἀντίθεος, η, ον godlike.
ἀντίος, η, ον to meet,
opposite, facing.
ἄντυξ, υγος f. rim.
ἄνωγα I order.
ἄξαντε aor. part. dual
of ἄγνυμι.
ἄξιος, α, ον fitting,
worthy.
ἄξον aor. imperative act.
of ἄγνυμι.
ἀοίδιμος, ον famed in
song.
ἀολλίζω gather together.
ἀπαμείβομαι answer.
ἅπας same as πᾶς.
ἀπαυράω take away.
ἄπειμι be absent, be away.

ἀπερείσιος, ον countless.
ἀπέσσυτο 3rd sing. 2nd.
aor. of ἀποσεύομαι.
ἀπεχθάνομαι (+ dat.) be
hateful (to).
ἀπέχω, aor. ἀπέσχον keep
away from.
ἀπηύρα 3rd sing. imperf.
of. ἀπαυράω.
ἀπιθέω (+ dat.) disobey.
ἀπό (+ gen.) from.
ἀποβαίνω go away.
ἀπογυιόω cripple; deprive
of (+ gen.).
ἀπόερσε aorist swept away.
ἄποινα n. pl. ransom.
ἀποκτείνω, 2nd aor. -έκτανον
kill.
ἀπολάμπω shine.
ἀπολήγω cease; wither.
ἀπόλλυμι destroy; (mid.)
perish.
ἀπολύω release.
ἀποπνείω breathe out.
ἀπορρήγνυμι break, snap.
ἀπορρήξας aor. part. of
ἀπορρήγνυμι.
ἀποσεύομαι speed away.
ἀπόσχῃ 3rd sing. aor. subj.
act. of ἀπέχω.
ἀπούρας aor. part. act. of
ἀπαυράω.
ἄρ, ἄρα indeed (often un-
translatable).
ἀράομαι pray.
ἀργεννός, ή, όν white.
ἀρέσκω make it up.
ἀρεσσόμεθα 1st pl. fut.
mid. of ἀρέσκω.
ἀρήιος, η, ον of war.
ἀρηίφιλος, ον loved by
Ares.
ἀριπρεπής, ές very distinguished.
ἀριστεύω to be best.
ἄριστος, η, ον best; most
valiant.
ἀρκέω, aor. ἤρκεσα ward off.
ἅρμα, ατος n. chariot.
ἄρνυμαι win; gain.
ἄρουρα, ης f. field, corn-
land.

ἀσπίς, ίδος f. shield.
ἄσσον adv. nearer.
ἀστερόεις, εντος starry.
ἀστήρ, έρος m. star.
ἄστυ, εος or ους or εως n.
city, town.
ἀταλάφρων, ον tender-minded.
ἀτάρ conj. but.
ἄτη, ης f. folly, madness.
ἀτιμάω disregard; slight.
ἄτος, ον for ἄατος (+ gen.)
insatiable (in).
ἀτύζομαι flee in terror.
ἀτυχθείς part. of
ἀτύζομαι: dismayed at.
αὖ adv. again.
αὐδάω speak.
αὖθι adv. here, on the
spot; straightway.
αὐλή, ῆς f. courtyard.
αὐτάρ conj. but,
besides.
αὖτε adv. then; again;
in turn; in reply.
ἀυτή, ῆς f. shouting;
battle-cry.
αὐτίκα adv. at once.
αὖτις adv. again.
αὐτός, ή, ό he, she, it;
self; same.
αὐτοῦ adv. there, here.
αὔτως adv. just, only.
αὐχήν, ένος m. neck.
ἀύω or ἀύω shout.
ἀφαμαρτάνω (+ gen.) lose.
ἄφαντος, ον unspoken of;
forgotten.
ἀφικάνω come to.
ἀφνειός, ή, όν rich (in).
ἀφάω or ἀφόω handle.
ἄχνυμαι be grieved at.
ἄχος, εος n. grief, de-
pression.
ἄψ adv. again, back again.

Β

βαίνω, perf. βέβηκα go,
step.
βάλλω strike, smite.

βασιλεύς, ῆος m. king.
βασιλεύω be king, be
queen.
βασιληίς, ίδος f. adj.
royal.
βῆ 3rd sing. aor. of
βαίνω, for ἔβη.
βήω aor. subj. of βαίνω,
for βῶ.
βίη, ης f. might, force.
βίοτος, ου m. means of
livelihood.
βλάπτω hinder, damage;
(pass.) break down.
βλώσκω, aor. ἔμολον come,
go.
βοή, ῆς f. battle-cry;
weeping.
βουλευτής, οῦ m. councillor.
βουπλήξ, ῆγος m. or f. ox-
goad.
βοῦς, βοός m. or. f. ox,
cow.
βροτόεις, εσσα, εν bloody.
βροτός, οῦ m. mortal
man.

Γ

γαῖα, ης f. earth, ground.
γάλοως, γάλοω sister-in-law,
husband's sister.
γαμβρός, οῦ m. son-in-law.
γάρ conj. for.
γαστήρ, έρος f. womb, belly.
γε particle at least (often
not translated).
γείνομαι am born; (aor.
trans.) bore.
γελάω laugh, smile.
γενεή, ῆς f. family, race,
birth.
γένος, εος n. race, family.
γεραιά, ᾶς f. old woman,
matron.
γέρων, οντος m. old man.
γηθέω rejoice.
γίγνομαι become, be, be
born, happen.
γιγνώσκω know, realise.

γλαυκῶπις, ιδος f. adj.
with gleaming eyes.
γνῶσιν 3rd pl. aor. subj.
of γιγνώσκω.
γοάω weep, mourn.
γόνος, ου m. offspring,
child.
γόνυ, γουνός n. knee.
γόος, ου m. lamentation.
γοῦνα pl. of γόνυ.
γούνασι dat. pl. of γόνυ.
γράφω scratch.
γυῖον, ου n. limb.
γυνή, γυναικός f. woman,
wife.

Δ

δαήμεναι inf. to know.
δαήρ, ἐρος m. brother-in-
law.
δαιδάλεος, ον richly wrought.
δαιμόνιε, δαιμονίη voc. my
dear man: dear lady (see
on 1.326).
δαίμων, ονος m. or f. god,
divinity.
δαΐφρων, ονος wise.
δάκρυ, υος n. tear.
δακρυόεις, εσσα, εν in
tears.
δακρυόεν adv. tearfully,
with tears.
δαμάω tame, subdue.
δαμέντες pl. aor. part.
pass. of δαμάω.
δαμόωσι 3rd pl. fut. of
δαμάω.
δέ particle (joining sen-
tences or phrases) and,
also, but.
δεδμημένος perf. part. pass.
of δέμω.
δειδιότα acc. sing. part.
of δείδω.
δείδω fear.
δείκνυμι show.
δεινόν adv. terribly,
dreadfully.
δεινός, ή, όν terrible,
dread.

δέκατος, η, ον tenth.
δέμω build.
δέξαι aor. imperative of
δέχομαι.
δέπας, αος n. cup.
δέρμα, ατος n. hide, skin.
δεσμός, οῦ m. halter.
δεῦρο adv. here, to this
place.
δεύτερον adv. secondly.
δέχομαι accept, receive.
δή (particle of emphasis)
indeed.
δηθύνω be long, tarry.
δήιος, ου m. enemy;
(as adj.) hostile.
δῆμος, ου m. people, land.
δήν adv. for a long time.
διά (+ gen.) through.
διδυμάονε dual twin.
δίδωμι give, grant.
διέξειμι go out through.
διεξίμεναι inf. of
διέξειμι.
διέρχομαι go through.
διίφιλος, ον dear to Zeus.
δῖος, δῖα, δῖον godlike,
noble, glorious.
δίφρος, ου m. car, chariot,
seat.
δμωή, ῆς f. handmaid.
δοκέω seem.
δολιχόσκιος, ον with a long
shaft.
δόλος, ου m. trick.
δόμος, ου m. house.
δόρυ, δούρατος or δουρός n.
spear.
δότε aor. imperative pl.
of δίδωμι.
δούλιος, η, ον of slavery.
δοῦρα pl. of δόρυ.
δράκων, οντος m. serpent.
δύμεναι 2nd aor. inf. of
δύω.
δύναμαι be able.
δύνηαι 2nd sing. pres. subj.
of δύναμαι.
δυοκαίδεκα twelve.
δύσετο 3rd sing. aor. of
δύω.
δυσμενής, ές hostile, enemy.

δύστηνος, ον wretched,
miserable.
δυσώνυμος, ον of evil
name.
δύω or δύνω go under,
plunge into; put on.
δύω two.
δώδεκα twelve.
δῶμα, ατος n. (often pl.)
house, chief hall.
δῶρον, ου n. gift.

E

ἔ, οὗ, οἷ (acc. gen. dat.)
he, she, it; himself, herself, itself.
ἔαρ, ἔαρος n. spring.
ἐβεβήκει 3rd sing. pluperf.
of βαίνω.
ἐβήτην 3rd dual aor. of
βαίνω.
ἐγγεγάασι 3rd pl. perf. of
ἐγγίγνομαι.
ἐγγίγνομαι be born in.
ἐγγύθι (+ gen.) near.
ἐγείρω rouse, stir up.
ἐγκλίνω bend to; (pass. +
dat.) rest on.
ἔγχος, εος n. spear.
ἐγώ or ἐγών I.
ἐδείδιμεν 1st pl. pluperf.
of δείδω.
ἐδύτην 2nd aor. dual of
δύω.
ἔδω eat.
ἐείκοσι twenty.
ἕζεο mid. imperative
of ἵζω.
ἐθέλω be willing, wish.
ἔθεν same as οὗ, gen.
of ἔ.
εἰ if.
εἰ (exclamation with
ἄγε) come now!
εἰδῇς 2nd sing. subj. of
οἶδα.
εἶδος, εος n. appearance,
beauty.
εἰδώς, υῖα, ός (+ gen.)
skilled in.
ἐικώς, υῖα, ός resembling,

like to.
εἵλετο 3rd sing. aor. mid.
of αἱρέω.
εἰλήλουθα 1st sing. perf.
of ἔρχομαι.
εἰλίπους, -ποδος with rol-
ling walk, shambling.
εἶμι go, come.
εἰμί be.
εἰνάτερες f. pl. sisters-
in-law; brothers' wives.
εἵνεκα (+ gen.) because of.
εἴπῃσι 3rd sing. aor. subj.
of λέγω.
εἴρομαι ask about.
εἰς (+ acc.) to, into.
εἷς, μία, ἕν one.
εἰσαναβαίνω go up into.
εἶσε 3rd sing. aor. of
ἵζω.
εἰσέρχομαι go in, enter.
εἴσω adv. within.
εἴσω (+ acc. or gen.)
into.
εἰωθώς perf. part.
accustomed.
ἐκ (+ gen.) out of,
from.
ἕκαστος, η, ον each.
ἑκατόμβη, ης f. public
sacrifice.
ἑκατόμβοιος, ον worth
100 oxen.
ἐκγελάω laugh out loud.
ἔκειτο 3rd sing. past
tense of κεῖμαι.
ἐκέκλετο 3rd sing. 2nd
aor. of κέλομαι.
ἔκηλος, ον at one's ease.
ἐκκυλίνδομαι roll out of.
ἐκλανθάνομαι forget.
ἐκλελαθέσθαι 2nd aor. inf.
mid. of ἐκλανθάνομαι.
ἐκπέρθω, aor. -περσα
destroy.
ἐκσπάω pull out.
ἔκτα 3rd sing. aor. of
κτείνω.
ἑκών, οῦσα, όν willingly.
ἔλασσεν 3rd sing. aor. of
ἐλαύνω.
ἐλαύνω drive.
ἐλεαίρω, ἐλεείνω, ἐλεέω pity.

ἐλελίζω rally.
ἐλεύθερος, ον free,
of freedom.
ἐλεύσομαι fut. of
ἔρχομαι.
ἑλκεσίπεπλος, ον long-
robed, with trailing
robes.
ἑλκηθμός, οῦ m. dragging
off, rough usage.
ἕλον aor. of αἱρέω (for
εἷλον).
ἐμός, ή, όν my.
ἔμπεδος, ον sound,
stable.
ἐμφύομαι, aor. ἐνέφυν
cling to.
ἐν (+ dat.) in, on.
ἐναίρω slay, kill.
ἐναίσιμον adv. at the
right time.
ἐναίσιμος, ον reasonable,
right-minded.
ἐναντίος, η, ον (+ gen.)
facing, opposite, to
meet.
ἔναρα n. pl. spoils,
booty.
ἐνδεκάπηχυς, υ eleven
cubits long.
ἔνδοθεν (+ gen.) within.
ἔνδοθι adv. within.
ἔνδον adv. at home,
within.
ἐνείκω 1st sing. aor.
subj. of φέρω.
ἔνειμι be in.
ἕνεκα (+ gen.) because
of.
ἐνέπω tell.
ἔνεσαν 3rd pl. imperf.
of ἔνειμι.
ἐνήρατο 3rd sing. aor.
mid. of ἐναίρω.
ἔνθα adv. there, then,
where.
ἔνθα καὶ ἔνθα this way and
that.
ἐνθάδε adv. here.
ἔνθεο 2nd sing. aor. indic.
of ἐντίθημι.
ἐνί (for ἐν) (+ dat.) in,

among.
ἔνισπε 3rd sing. aor. of
ἐνέπω.
ἐννέα nine.
ἐννεάβοιος, ον worth
nine oxen.
ἐννῆμαρ adv. for nine
days.
ἐνόρνυμι stir up.
ἔντεα n. pl. arms, weapons,
armour.
ἐντίθημι keep in, place in.
ἔντοσθεν (+ gen.) within.
ἐντροπαλίζομαι look back.
ἐνῶρσεν 3rd sing. aor. of
ἐνόρνυμι.
ἐξ (same as ἐκ) out of,
from.
ἐξαιρέω take away.
ἐξαπόλλυμι destroy utterly;
(mid.) perish utterly.
ἐξείης adv. one after the
other, in order.
ἐξέλετο 3rd sing. aor. mid.
of ἐξαιρέω.
ἐξεναρίζω slay; strip of
armour.
ἐξοίχομαι have gone out.
ἐξονομάζω call by name,
address.
ἔξοχος, ον (+ gen.) super-
ior (to).
ἐπαμείβομαι exchange; alter-
nate between.
ἐπαμύνω (+ dat.) help.
ἐπαυρίσκομαι fut. -αυρήσομαι
reap the fruits of.
ἐπεί conj. since, when.
ἐπείγω press upon; (mid.)
hasten.
ἔπειτα adv. next, then.
ἐπέσσυται 3rd sing. perf.
of ἐπισεύω.
ἐπεύχομαι (+ dat.) pray to.
ἔπεφνε 3rd sing. aor. of
φένω.
ἐπήν conj. when.
ἐπί (+ dat.) on, over, at,
against, in, in charge of.
(+ acc.) onto, to, over,
for.
ἐπιβάλλομαι (+ gen.) throw

oneself on.
ἐπιγίγνομαι follow,
come after.
ἐπίδρομος, ον assailable.
ἐπίκειμαι lie upon (trans.).
ἐπίκουρος, ου m. ally.
ἐπιμαίνομαι, aor. ἐπεμηνάμην
(+ dat.) be madly in love
with.
ἐπιμένω wait.
ἐπιπλέω sail over.
ἐπιπλώς aor. part of
ἐπιπλέω.
ἐπισεύω be eager, hasten.
ἐπίσπης 2nd sing. aor. subj.
of ἐφέπω.
ἐπιτέλλω order, command.
ἐπιτίθημι set on.
ἐπιχέω pour over, heap
upon.
ἔπλετο 3rd sing. imperf.
of πέλομαι.
ἐποίχομαι go round, go up
and down, attend to.
ἔπος, εος n. word, speech.
ἐποτρύνω rouse, urge on.
ἐπουράνιος, η, ον heavenly.
ἔπτα seven.
ἔπω attend to, handle.
ἐρατεινός, ή, όν lovely,
to be desired.
ἔργον, ου n. work, deed,
effort.
ἐρεείνω question, ask
(about).
ἐρέω fut. indic. of
λέγω.
ἐριβῶλαξ, ακος with rich
soil.
ἐρίζω (+ dat.) strive
with.
ἐρινεός, ου m. fig-tree.
ἕρκος, εος n. bulwark,
defence.
ἐρύκω, aor. ἐρύκακον/ἔρυξα
keep, control, detain
(as a guest).
ἔρχεο 2nd sing. imperative
of ἔρχομαι.
ἔρχομαι come, go.
ἐς (+ acc.) same as εἰς:
to, into.

ἐσάγω bring in.
ἐσθλός, ή, όν brave, good.
ἔσκε (for ἦν): he was.
ἐσσύμενος, η, ον hurrying.
ἔσταν 3rd pl. aor. of
ἵσταμαι.
ἔστι it is possible.
ἑταῖρος or ἕταρος, ου m.
comrade.
ἑτέρωθεν adv. on the other
side.
ἔτετμεν aor. (no pres.)
he overtook.
ἔτης, ου m. friend, kins-
man.
ἔτι adv. any longer, still,
again.
ἐΰ or εὖ adv. well.
ἐΰζωνος, ον well-girdled.
ἐϋκνήμις, ιδος well-greaved.
ἐϋκτίμενος, η, ον well-
built.
ἐϋμμελίης, gen. -ω armed
with ashen spear.
εὐνή, ῆς f. bed, marriage-
bed.
εὐπατέρεια f. adj. high-
born.
ἐΰπεπλος, ον fair-robed.
ἐϋπλόκαμος, ον with fair
tresses.
ἐϋρρεής, ές fair-flowing.
εὑρίσκω, aor. εὗρον find.
ἐϋρρεῖος gen. sing. of
ἐϋρρεής.
ἐϋρρείτης, αο fair-flowing.
εὐρύς, εῖα, ύ broad, wide.
ἐΰς or ἠΰς noble, brave.
εὖτε conj. when.
εὐχετάομαι pray.
εὔχομαι boast, pray, claim
(to be).
ἔφαντο 3rd pl. aor. mid.
of φημί.
ἐφάπτομαι attach to.
ἔφατο 3rd sing. aor. of
φημί.
ἐφέπω meet with, come to.
ἐφεστήκει (+ dat.) was
standing on (from ἐφίσταμαι).
ἐφῆπτο 3rd sing. pluperf.
pass of ἐφάπτομαι.

ἐφορμάομαι rush upon, attack.
ἔχω have, hold; (pass.) be married to.

Z

ζωγρέω take alive.
ζωός, ἥ, όν alive.
ζωστήρ, ῆρος m. belt.
ζώω live.

H

ἤ particle truly, indeed.
ἦ he/she spoke.
ἤ or
ἤ ... ἤ or ἤ ... ἤ either ... or.
ἦ interrogative can it be that?
ᾗ in which direction, where?
ἠγάθεος, η, ον holy, hallowed.
ἠδέ conj. and.
ᾔδη pluperf. (imperf. sense) of οἶδα.
ἤδη adv. now, already.
ἠέ for ἤ
ἤθεα n. pl. haunts, abodes.
ἠθεῖος, η, ον respected; (in voc.) see on 1. 518.
ἠκέστας acc. pl. unbroken.
ἠλακάτη, ης f. distaff.
ἠλέκτωρ, ορος m. sun.
ἤλυθον for ἦλθον.
ἧμαι sit.
ἦμαρ, ἤματος n. day.
ἡμέτερος, η, ον our.
ἤμην 1st sing. imperf. of ἧμαι.
ἤμισυ n. half.
ἤνις acc. pl. yearlings.
ἠνορέη, ης f. manliness.
ἠνώγει 3rd sing. pluperf. of ἄνωγα (with imperf. sense).
ἠπιόδωρος, ον graciously

giving, generous.
ἥρως, ωος m. hero, warrior.
ἧστο 3rd sing. past tense of ἧμαι.
ἦτορ n. heart.
ηὔδα 3rd sing. imperf. of αὐδάω.
ἠύκομος, ον fair-haired, with beautiful hair.
ἠύς (also ἐύς) noble, brave.

Θ

θάλαμος, ου m. room.
θάλασσα, ης f. sea.
θαλερός, ἥ, όν goodly, vigorous; (with δάκρυ) big.
θαλπωρή, ῆς f. comfort.
θάρσος, ους n. courage, daring.
θᾶσσον adv. more quickly.
θεά, ᾶς f. goddess.
θείη for θέῃ 3rd sing. subj. of θέω.
θείνω strike.
θεῖος, η, ον divine.
θεοειδής, ές godlike.
θεοπρόπιον, ου n. oracle.
θεός, ου m. or f. god, goddess.
θεράπων, οντος m. attendant, squire.
θέρομαι be burned.
θές 2nd sing. aor. imperative of τίθημι.
θέω run.
θήῃς 2nd sing. aor. subj. of τίθημι.
θνήσκω die.
θοός, ἥ, όν swift.
θοῦρις, ιδος adj. impetuous.
θρασύς, εῖα, ύ spirited, bold.
θυγάτηρ, έρος f. daughter.
θύελλα, ης f. storm.
θυμός, οῦ m. life, heart, mind, desire, courage, breath.
θυμοφθόρος, ον deadly.

θύος, εος n. sacrifice.
θύρη, ης f. door.
θύσθλα, ων n. pl. Bacchic
implements of worship.
θώρηξ, ηκος m. breast-
plate.

I

ἰάχω cry.
ἰδέ conj. and.
ἰδέσθαι aor. inf. mid. of
δράω.
ἴδωμαι 1st sing. aor. subj.
mid. of δράω.
ἰέρεια f. priestess.
ἰερεύω sacrifice.
ἰερός, ή, όν sacred, holy.
ἴζω place, set; (mid.)
sit.
ἰθύνομαι (+ gen.) aim at.
ἰθύς, ύος f. enterprise.
ἰθύω go straight, advance.
ἰκάνω, ἰκνέομαι come,
arrive at.
ἵκω, aor. ἵξον come,
arrive at.
ἱλάσκομαι placate,
appease.
ἵξε 3rd sing. aor. of
ἵκω.
ἵος, ἵα one.
ἰοχέαιρα archer, pouring
arrows.
ἱππιοχαίτης, ου of horse-
hair.
ἱππόβοτος, ον horse-
rearing.
ἱππόδαμος, ον horse-
taming.
ἱπποδάσεια f. adj. with
horse-hair plume.
ἵππος, ου m. or f. horse,
mare; (in pl.) chariot.
ἵππουρις, ιδος with horse-
hair plume.
ἱρός, ή, όν (for ἱερός)
sacred.
ἰσοφαρίζω (+ dat.) match,
be equal to.
ἵσταμαι stand.

ἵστημι, aor. ἔστησα place,
set.
ἱστός, οῦ m. loom.
ἶφι dat. with might.

K

καγχαλάω laugh aloud.
καθίζω make to sit.
καί conj. and adv. and,
also, even.
κακομήχανος, ον mischievous.
κακός, ή, όν evil, bad,
cowardly.
κάκτανε for κατάκτανε
(κατακτείνω).
καλά adv. well.
καλέω call.
καλλιπάρηος, ον with fair
cheeks.
κάλλος, εος n. beauty.
καλός, ή, όν fine, fair,
beautiful.
καλύπτω cover.
κάμνω be weary.
κάπ for κατά.
κάρη, κρατός n. head.
καρπός, οῦ m. fruit.
κάρτιστος, η, ον mightiest.
κασίγνητος, ου m. brother.
κατά (+ acc.) in, throughout, down to, along,
below. (+ gen.) down from.
καταβαίνω go down.
κατάγω lead back.
καταδύω put on.
καταθνητός, όν mortal.
κατακαίω, aor. κατέκηα burn,
cremate.
κατακαλύπτω cover.
κατακτείνω kill.
καταλείπω leave behind.
καταμάρπτω overtake.
καταπήγνυμι, aor. -πηξα fix
firmly.
καταρέζω, aor. -ερεξα stroke,
caress.
κατατίθημι set down.
καταφένω slay.
καταχέω fling down, shed,
pour down.

κατεβήσετο 3rd sing. aor.
mid. of καταβαίνω.
κατέδυ 3rd sing. aor. of
καταδύω.
κατέδω eat up, devour.
κατέκτανον 2nd aor. of
κατακτείνω.
κατέπεφνε 3rd sing. aor.
of καταφένω.
κατερύκω detain, keep.
κατέρχομαι come down;
go down.
κε(ν) particle (used
in potential, hypothetical
or indefinite clauses)
same meaning as ἄν.
κεῖμαι lie (down).
κειμήλιον, ου n. treasure.
κεῖνος, κείνη, κεῖνο he,
she, it; that.
κέκλετο aor. of κέλομαι.
κέκμηκας 2nd sing. perf.
act. of κάμνω.
κεκμηῶτι dat. sing. m. perf.
part. of κάμνω.
κελαινεφής, ές shrouded in
black clouds.
κελαινός, ή, όν black.
κελεύω (+ dat. or acc.)
order.
κέλομαι (+ acc. or dat.)
call, urge on.
κέρδιστος, η, ον most
cunning.
κερδίων, ον better.
κήδομαι (+ gen.) care
about.
κῆδος, εος n. sorrow,
trouble.
κῆρ n. heart.
κηώδης, ες fragrant,
sweet-smelling.
κηώεις, εσσα, εν fragrant.
κιχάνω meet with, find,
overtake.
κιχείω 1st pers. subj.
act. of κιχάνω.
κιχήσατο 3rd sing. aor. of
κιχάνω.
κιχήσεσθαι fut. inf. of
κιχάνω.
κίω go.

κλειτός, ή, όν famous.
κλέος n. glory, fame.
κληΐς, κληΐδος f. key.
κλίνομαι lean.
κλυτός, ή, όν famous,
glorious.
κοιμάομαι sleep.
κόλπος, ου m. bosom.
κομίζω attend to.
κονίη, ης (or pl.) f.
dust.
κορυθαίολος, ον with
shining helmet.
κόρυς, κόρυθος f. helmet.
κούρη, ης f. daughter.
κοῦρος, ου m. boy, son.
κραιπνός, ή, όν swift.
κρατερός, ή, όν mighty,
strong.
κράτιστος superlative
of κράτερος.
κράτος, εος n. might,
strength.
κρατός gen. of κάρη.
κρείων lord.
κρητήρ, ῆρος m. bowl.
κρίνω choose out.
κροαίνω stamp, clatter.
κρυόεις, εσσα, εν icy-cold,
chilling.
κρυπτάδιος, η, ον secret.
κτέαρ, κτέατος n. posses-
sion.
κτείνω kill.
κυδάλιμος, ον famous, re-
nowned.
κυδιάνειρα f. adj. that
gives men fame.
κυδιάω exult.
κῦμα, ατος n. wave.
κυνέω, aor. κύσα kiss.
κύων, κυνός m. and f.
dog, bitch.

Λ

λαμβάνω take, catch hold of,
receive.
λάμπω shine.
λανθάνομαι (+ gen.) forget.
λάξ adv. with the heel.

λαός, οῦ m. people, army.
λαπάρη, ης f. flank,
  loins.
λέγω, aor. εἶπον or εἶπα
  say, speak.
λείβω pour (as a libation).
λείπω leave.
λευκώλενος, ον white-armed.
λέων, οντος m. lion.
λήγω (+ gen.) cease from.
λῆξαν 3rd pl. aor. act.
  of λήγω.
λιήν adv. overmuch,
  very much.
λίθος, ου m. stone.
λίσσομαι pray, implore.
λούομαι bathe.
λόφος, ου m. plume.
λόχος, ου m. ambush.
λυγρός, ή, όν sad, grievous,
  fatal (see on 1. 168).
λύθρος, ου m. filth, gore.
λωίων, ον better.

M

μαίνομαι rage, be furious,
  be wild, be mad.
μάκαρ, μάκαρος blessed.
μακρόν adv. loudly.
μακρός, ή, όν long, great.
μάλα adv. very, very
  much.
μαλακός, ή, όν soft,
  gentle.
μάλιστα adv. most; (+ gen.)
  most among, especially.
μανθάνω learn, be taught.
μάρναμαι (+ dat.) fight.
μάχη, ης f. battle.
μάχομαι (+ dat.) fight
  against, fight.
μέγα adv. by far,
  greatly.
μεγάθυμος, ον high-minded.
μεγαλήτωρ, ορος great-
  hearted.
μέγαρον, ου n. hall,
  shrine; (in pl.) palace.
μέγας, μεγάλη, μέγα big,
  mighty.

μεθίημι (+ gen.) slacken,
  be slack in.
μειδάω smile.
μείλινος or μέλινος, η, ον
  of ash-wood.
μειλίχιος, ον gentle.
μελιηδής, ές honey-sweet.
μελίφρων, ονος delicious.
μέλλω intend, be about
  to.
μέλω be a care to.
μεμαώς, ῶτος eager.
μέμνημαι remember.
μέν introduces the first of
  two connected clauses; usually answered by δέ.
μενεπτόλεμος, ον staunch
  in battle.
μένος, εος n. courage,
  strength, force.
μένω remain; (trans.) wait
  for, expect.
μέσον, ου n. middle.
μεσσηγύ(ς) (+ gen.)
  between.
μέσσος, η, ον middle, in
  the middle.
μετά (+ acc.) in pursuit of,
  in search of; (+ dat.)
  among.
μετασεύομαι hurry after.
μέτειμι fut. come after.
μετεῖπον aor. spoke to.
μετέρχομαι, fut. -ελεύσομαι
  go to, go to find.
μετόπισθε(ν) adv. behind.
μέτωπον, ου n. forehead.
μή negative in certain con-
  structions.
μηδέ not even, and not.
μήδομαι, aor. ἐμησάμην
  devise; (+ acc. and dat.)
  plot (x) against (y), see
  1. 157.
μήστωρ, ωρος m. deviser.
μήτηρ, ερος / ρός f. mother.
μητίετα, ου m. counsellor.
μίγη 3rd sing. 2nd aor. of
  μίγνυμι.
μιγήμεναι 2nd aor. inf. pass.
  of μίγνυμι.
μίγνυμι mingle, join.

μιμνήσκω (+ gen.)
remember.
μίμνω (for μένω) stay,
remain.
μιν acc. him, her, it;
them.
μνήσασθε aor. imperative
mid. of μιμνήσκω.
μνηστός, ή, όν wedded.
μοῖρα, ης f. fate.
μολοῦσα f. sing. aor.
part. of βλώσκω.
μόρος, ου m. destiny.
μυθέομαι speak, tell.
μῦθος, ου m. word.
μυρίκινος, η, ον of
tamarisk.
μύρομαι wail.
μυχός, οῦ m. corner.

N

ναιετάω dwell, see on l.
370.
ναίω dwell (intrans.); live
in (trans.).
νείατος, η, ον lowest.
νεικέω reproach, taunt.
νεκρός, οῦ m. corpse.
νέμεσις, εως f. annoyance,
indignation.
νέμομαι occupy, possess.
νέομαι go, come, return.
νέος, η, ον new.
νεύω nod, wave.
νηίς, ίδος f. water nymph.
νημερτής, ές true.
νηός, οῦ m. temple.
νηπίαχος same as νήπιος.
νήπιος, η, ον infant.
νηῦς, νηός, dat. pl. νηυσί
f. ship.
νίκη, ης f. victory.
νιν same as μιν.
νοέω notice, perceive.
νομός, οῦ m. pasture-
ground.
νόσφιν (+ gen.) far from.
νύ particle then.
νύμφη, ης f. nymph.
νῦν adv. now.

Ξ

ξεινήια n. pl. friendly
gifts.
ξεινίζω entertain.
ξεῖνος, ου m. friend,
guest, host.
ξεστός, ή, όν polished.
ξύν same as σύν.
ξυνάγω gather together.

Ο

ὁ, ἡ, τό he, she, it; the;
who.
ὅ for ὅς (see on l. 153).
ὀαρίζω talk intimately.
ὅδε, ἥδε, τόδε this.
ὁδός, οῦ f. road,
journey.
ὀδύσσομαι (+ dat.) be
angry (with).
δεσσι or ὁίεσσι dat. pl.
of ὄις.
ὄζος, ου m. branch.
ὅθι where.
οἱ dat. of ἑ from/to him,
her, it; his.
οἴγω, aor. ᾦξα or ὦιξα open.
οἶδα know, be aware of.
ὀιζύς, ύος f. woe, distress.
οἰκεύς, ῆος m. inmate of a
house.
οἰκία n. pl. house.
οἶκος, ου m. house, home.
οἶνος, ου m. wine.
οἶος, η, ον alone.
οἷος, η, ον such, as.
οἰόω leave alone.
ὄις m. and f. sheep.
οἴχομαι go.
ὀίω think.
οἰωνοπόλος, ου m. seer,
prophet.
ὄλεθρος, ου m. death,
destruction.
ὄλλυμι destroy; (mid.)
perish.
ὀλολυγή, ῆς f. a loud cry.
ὄλωλα perish.
ὅμιλος, ου m. throng of

battle.
ὀμοκλέω call, shout to.
ὀμοκλή, ῆς f. shouting.
ὀμφαλόεις, εσσα, εν with a
central boss.
ὀνήσεαι 2nd sing. aor. subj.
of ὀνίναμαι.
ὀνήσομαι fut. of ὀνίναμαι.
ὀνίναμαι mid. refresh
oneself.
ὀξύς, εῖα, ύ sharp.
ὀπάζω bestow, grant.
ὄπιθεν adv. behind.
ὄπισθεν adv. hereafter.
ὀπίσσω adv. behind,
hereafter.
ὄπωπα have seen.
ὀράω see, look (at).
ὀρέγομαι, aor. ὀρεξάμην
(+ gen.) reach out for.
ὀρεστιάς f. adj. of the
mountains.
ὀρμάω urge, speed (trans.).
ὄρνυμι, imperative ὄρνυθι
rouse.
ὄρος, εος n. mountain.
ὀρφανικός, ή, όν orphaned.
ὄρχαμος, ου m. marshal.
ὅς, ἥ, ὅ rel. pron. who,
what; which.
ὅς demonstrative he.
ὅς, ἥ, ὅν his, her.
ὄσσε dual n. eyes.
ὄσσος, η, ον how great,
so great.
ὀστέον, ου n. bone.
ὅστις, ὅττι or ὅς τις, ὅ τι
whoever, whatever.
ὅτε conj. when.
ὅτι conj. that.
ὀτρηρός, ή, όν busy,
zealous.
ὀτρύνω rouse, urge on.
ὅττι see ὅστις.
οὐ, οὐκ, οὐχ not.
οὐδέ adv. not even, nor,
and ... not.
οὐδός, οῦ m. threshold.
οὕνεκα conj. because.
οὐρανός, οῦ m. heaven, sky.
οὐτάω wound, stab.
οὔτε ... οὔτε neither ... nor.

οὗτος, αὕτη, τοῦτο this.
οὕτω(ς) so, thus.
ὀφείλω, aor. ὄφελον, ὤφελλον
owe, ought.
ὄφελε 3rd sing. aor. of
ὀφείλω.
ὄφρα conj. until; in order
that.
ὄχ' by far.
ὄχθη, ης f. bank (of a
river).
ὄχος, εος n. (usually pl.)
chariot.
ὄψις, ιος f. appearance.

Π

πάϊς / παῖς, παιδός m. or f.
child, son, daughter.
παλαιός, ή, όν old, of old
times.
παλάσσω bespatter.
πάλιν adv. again.
πάλλω brandish, shake,
toss.
παμποίκιλος, ον richly
embroidered.
παμφαίνω shine brightly.
παμφανόων, όωσα all-
shining.
πάντη adv. everywhere.
παρά (+ acc.) beside.
(+ gen.) from, (+ dat.)
beside.
παραδέχομαι receive (from).
παρακοίτης, ου m. husband.
παραλέγομαι, -λεξάμην (+ dat.)
lie with.
παραπείθω win over.
παραστάς aor. part. of
παρίσταμαι.
παρειπεῖν persuade.
παρίσταμαι (+ dat.) stand
beside.
πάροιθε (+ gen.) in front
of.
πάρος conj. before.
πᾶς, πᾶσα, πᾶν all.
πατήρ, πατρός m. father.
πάτος, ου m. path, track.
πατρώιος, η, ον of a father,

coming from a father.
πεδίον, ου *n.* plain.
πείθω persuade.
πεῖραρ, πείρατος *n.* end
  (*see on* 1. 143).
πειράομαι try, make an
  attempt.
πέλομαι be, become.
πέμπω send.
πενθερός, οῦ *m.* father-
  in-law.
πεντήκοντα fifty.
πεπαλαγμένον *perf. part.*
  pass. of παλάσσω.
πέπλος, ου *m.* robe.
πεποιθώς (+ *dat.*) trusting
  in.
πεπύθοιτο *3rd sing. 2nd aor.*
  opt. of πυνθάνομαι.
πέπον *vocative* my dear
  fellow.
περ *particle of emphasis*
  (*with part.*) although.
περάω pass through.
περί (+ *acc.*) around,
  (*as adv.*) around.
περικαλλής, ές very
  beautiful.
περικλυτός, ή, όν excel-
  lent, wondrous.
πεφνέμεν *aor. inf. of*
  φένω.
πεφυγμένος, η, ον *part.*
  having escaped.
πῇ; which way?
πη *adv.* at all, in any
  way.
πήγνυμι stick in.
πῆλε *3rd sing. aor. of*
  πάλλω.
πῆμα, ατος *n.* trouble,
  bane.
πῆξε *3rd sing. aor. of*
  πήγνυμι.
πίησθα *2nd sing. aor.*
  subj. mid. of πίνω.
πιθέω (+ *dat.*) obey.
πίναξ, πίνακος *m.* tablet.
πίνω drink.
πίπτω fall.
πιστόομαι exchange pledges.
πλησίον (+ *gen.*) near.

ποδάρκης, ες fleet-footed.
ποθή, ῆς *f.* desire,
  longing (for).
ποθι *same as* ποτε.
ποιέω do, make.
ποίκιλμα, ατος *n.*
  embroidery.
ποικίλος, η, ον adorned.
ποιμαίνω be a shepherd.
ποιμήν, ένος shepherd.
πολέες *for* πολλοί: many.
πόλεμος, ου *m.* war.
πόλις, ιος *f.* city.
πολλά *adv.* much.
πολλόν *same as* πολύ.
πολύ *adv.* very, much,
  by far.
πολύδωρος, ον well-dowered.
πολύκμητος, ον difficult
  to work.
πολύς, πολλή, πολύ much,
  many.
πολύφλοισβος, ον loud-
  roaring.
πομπή, ῆς *f.* escort.
πόνος, ου *m.* trouble, toil.
πόντος, ου *m.* sea.
πόρκης, ου *m.* ring.
πόρον *same as* ἔπορον *aor.*
  provided, gave.
πόσις, ιος *m.* husband.
ποσσί *epic dat. pl. of*
  πούς.
ποταμός, οῦ *m.* river.
ποτε *adv.* once, ever,
  some day.
ποτί *same as* πρός.
πότμος, ου *m.* fate, doom.
πότνια *f. adj.* lady,
  mistress.
που *adv.* anywhere, some-
  where; no doubt.
πουλυβοτείρη *f. adj.* rich-
  nurturing.
πούς, ποδός *m.* foot.
πρεσβύτατος, η, ον eldest.
πρηνής, ές head-first.
πρίν *conj. and adv.* before,
  previously.
πρό (+ *gen.*) in front of.
προβαίνω (+ *gen.*) go in
  front of, surpass.

προιάπτω send before the
time.
προπάροιθε (+ gen.) in
front of.
πρός (+ acc.) to, towards:
(+ gen.) by, at the
hands of, at the orders
of.
προσαυδάω speak to.
προσειπεῖν speak to,
speak.
προσέφην spoke to.
πρόσθε(ν) adv. in front.
πρότερος, η, ον first (of
two).
προτί same as πρός.
προτρέπομαι yield to.
προφέρω carry away.
προφεύγω escape.
προφρονέως adv. readily,
willingly.
πρῶτον or πρῶτα adv.
first.
πρῶτος, η, ον first,
front part of.
πτελέη, ης f. elm-tree.
πτόλεμος same as πόλεμος.
πτόλις same as πόλις.
πτυκτός, όν folded.
πυκινός, ή, όν cunning.
πύλη, ης f. gate.
πύματος, η, ον outer.
πυνθάνομαι learn, hear
of, find out.
πῦρ, πυρός n. fire.
πύργος, ου m. tower.

P

ῥα or ῥ' see ἄρα.
ῥεῖα adv. easily, without
care.
ῥέω flow.
ῥήγνυμι break.
ῥῆξε 3rd sing. aor. of
ῥήγνυμι.
ῥίμφα adv. lightly.
ῥοδοδάκτυλος, ον rosy-
fingered.
ῥοή, ῆς f. stream,
river.

ῥυμός, οῦ m. chariot-
pole.
ῥύομαι defend.
ῥυσίπτολις protector of
the city.

Σ

σεβάζομαι feel awe at,
dread.
σεῖο, σεῦ or σέθεν for
σοῦ (from σύ).
σεύατο 3rd sing. aor. mid.
of σεύω.
σεύω chase; (mid.) rush.
σῆμα, ατος n. sign, token;
funeral mound.
σίδηρος, ου m. iron.
σιωπή, ῆς f. silence.
σκῆπτρον, ου n. sceptre,
staff.
σκότιος, ον in secret.
σκότος, ου m. darkness.
σός, ή, όν your.
σπένδω, aor. ἔσπεισα pour
a libation.
στατός, ή, όν stalled.
στῆθος, εος n. breast,
heart.
στήσασθαι aor. inf. mid.
of ἴστημι.
στῆτε pl. aor. imperative
of ἴσταμαι.
στόμα, ατος n. mouth.
στρατός, οῦ m. army.
στρέφομαι turn.
στυγερός, ή, όν hateful.
συλάω strip.
σύ pronoun. you (sing.).
σύν (+ dat.) with.
συνάγω gather together.
σύνειμι come together.
σύνθεο aor. imperative of
συντίθημι.
συνίτην dual imperf. of
σύνειμι.
συντίθημι take heed.
σφιν to them, for them.
σφυρόν, οῦ n. ankle.
σχεδόν adv. nearly, near.

T

ταί *same as* αἱ: they.
ταμίη, ης *f.* housekeeper.
τάμον *aor. of* τέμνω.
ταρβέω fear.
τάχα *adv.* quickly, soon.
ταχύς, εῖα, ύ swift.
-τε and, also.
τε ... τε *or* τε ... καί
  both ... and.
τέγεος, ον roofed.
τεθναίης *2nd sing. perf. opt.
  of* θνήσκω.
τεθνηώς, ῶτος *perf. part. of*
  θνήσκω: dead.
τείρω wear, wear out,
  press hard.
τεῖχος, εος *n.* wall.
τέκε *3rd sing. aor. of*
  τίκτω.
τέκετο *3rd sing. aor. of*
  τίκτομαι.
τεκμαίρομαι decree.
τέκνον, ου *n.* child.
τέκτων, ονος *m.* crafts-
  man.
τέμενος, εος *n.* domain,
  piece of land.
τέμνω, *aor.* ἔταμον cut
  off.
τέρας, τέρα(τ)ος *n.* sign.
τέτμεν *aor.* (he) found.
τεύχεα *n. pl.* weapons,
  arms.
τεύχω make, build.
τῇ by which way; at this
  point (*see on l.* 393).
τετυγμένον *perf. part.
  pass. of* τεύχω.
τέτυκτο *3rd sing. pluperf.
  pass. of* τεύχω.
τηλεθόωσα *part. of* τηλεθάω:
  flourishing.
τηλεκλειτός, όν far-famed.
τί ἦ *or* τίη; why?
τίθημι, *aor. inf.* θεῖναι
  place, put; make; bring.
τιθήνη, ης *f.* nurse.
τίκτω *or* τίκτομαι bear, give
  birth to, beget.
τιμή, ῆς *f.* honour,
τίπτε (τί ποτε); why ever?,
  why?
τις, τι anyone, anything;
  someone, something.
τίς; τί; who?, what?
τίω honour.
τοι *emphatic particle.*
τοι *same as* σοι.
τοί *for* οἱ they.
τοῖος, η, ον such, so
  (*following* οἷος *l.* 146).
τοιόσδε, -ήδε, -όνδε such.
τόξον, ου *n. and pl.* bow.
τόσσον *adv.* so much.
τόσσον ... ὅσσον so much
  ... as.
τότε *adv.* then.
τοὔνεκα *adv.* therefore.
τρεῖς, τρία three.
τρέφω rear.
τρίς *adv.* three times.
τρίτον, τό *adv.* thirdly.
τρόμος, ου *m.* trembling.
τροχός, οῦ wheel.
τύνη *same as* σύ.
τύπτω hit, strike.
τυτθός, όν small, young.
τυφλός, ή, όν blind.
τῶ *adv.* therefore.
τώ *dual.* the two of them.

Y

ὕδωρ, ατος *n.* water.
υἱός, οῦ *m.* (*pl.* υἶες) son.
ὕλη, ης *f.* forest.
ὑλήεις, εσσα, εν wooded.
ὔμμι *same as* ὑμῖν.
ὑπαντιάζω go to meet.
ὑπείροχος, ον (+ *gen.*)
  better than, preeminent.
ὑπεκφεύγω escape from.
ὑπέρ (+ *acc.*) beyond (*see on
  ll.* 333, 487) (+ *gen.*)
  about, concerning.
ὑπέρθυμος, ον high-spirited.
ὑπισχνέομαι promise.
ὑπό (+ *gen.*) by, by means
  of, at the hands of; (+ *dat.*)
  under, at the hands of.
ὑποδέχομαι receive.
ὑποκύομαι become pregnant.
ὑπολύω loosen, slacken.

ὑποπλάκιος, η, ον under
Mt. Plakos.
ὑπότροπος, ον returning
home.
ὑποχωρέω give way.
ὑφαίνω devise, work at,
ply.
ὑφηνίοχος, ου m. chariot-
eer, driver.
ὑψηλός, ή, όν high, lofty.
ὑψίπυλος, ον with high
gates.
ὑψοῦ adv. high.

Φ

φαεινός, ή, όν shining.
φαίδιμος, ον famous,
glorious.
φαίην opt. of φημί.
φαίνομαι appear.
φάλαγξ, αγγος f. battle-
line.
φάλος, ου m. see on l. 9.
φάν for ἔφησαν (3rd pl.
aor. of φημί).
φάος, φάεος n. light,
deliverance.
φάτνη, ης f. manger.
φάτο 3rd sing. aor. of
φημί.
φένω slay.
φέριστος (usually voc.)
bravest, very brave.
φέρτερος, α, ον stronger.
φέρω carry, bear, bring.
φεύγω flee, escape.
φηγός, οῦ f. oak-tree.
φημί say, speak.
φθινύθω perish.
φθίω destroy.
φιλέεσκον frequentative
imperf. of φιλέω.
φιλέω entertain, love,
welcome.
φίλος, η, ον dear; one's
own.
φίλος, ου m. friend.
φιλότης, ητος f. love-
making (see on l. 25).
φοβέομαι flee in terror.

φόβος, ου m. fear.
φοῖνιξ, ικος m. crimson
(dye).
φόνος, ου m. slaughter.
φορέω carry.
φόως see φάος.
φρήν, φρενός f. mind, heart;
(pl.) senses.
φρονέω think, plan, be
minded.
φῦ with ἐν see ἐμφύομαι.
φύλλον, ου n. leaf.
φύλοπις, ιδος f. din of
battle, battle.
φυταλιή, ῆς f. vineyard.
φυτεύω plant.
φύω produce, come forth,
flourish (see on l. 149).
φωνέω speak.
φώς, φωτός m. man.

Χ

χαίνω, aor. ἔχανον gape
open.
χαίρω, aor. ἐχάρην rejoice.
χαίτη, ης f. mane (often
pl.).
χάλκειος, η, ον of bronze.
χαλκήρης, ες bronze-tipped.
χαλκοκορυστής, οῦ m. adj.
with bronze helmet.
χαλκός, οῦ m. bronze.
χαλκοχίτων, ωνος bronze-clad.
χαμάδις adv. on the ground.
χαμᾶζε adv. to the ground.
χαμαί adv. on the ground.
χάνοι 3rd sing. aor. opt. of
χαίνω.
χαρείη 3rd sing. aor. opt.
of χαίρω.
χαρίεις, εσσα, εν elegant,
beautiful.
χαρίζομαι give, bestow.
χάρμα, ατος n. source of
joy.
χείρ, χειρός or χερός hand,
arm.
χέω pour, scatter, shed.
χήρη, ης f. widow.
χῆτος, εος n. lack.

χθών, χθονός f. ground,
  earth.
χίμαιρα, ης f. she-goat.
χολόομαι be angry.
χόλος, ου m. anger.
χρύσεος, η, ον golden.
χρυσήνιος, ον with golden
  reins.
χρυσός, οῦ m. gold.
χυτός, ή, όν heaped up,
  high-piled.
χώρη, ης f. place.

Ψ

ψεύδομαι lie, tell lies.

Ω

ὤ *particle introducing*
  a voc.
ὧδε *adv.* thus, so.
ὠθέω push.
ὦμος, ου m. shoulder.
ὥρη, ης f. season.
ὥς *adv.* thus.
ὡς as, since, when;
  (*exclamatory*) how!
ὡς (+ *acc.*) to.
ὡς or ὥς κε in order that.
ὤσατο *3rd sing. aor. mid.*
  of ὠθέω.
ὤφελλον *see* ὀφειλω.

PROPER NAMES

Note: People and places about which little or nothing is known are not listed. Of those listed only facts relevant to Book Six are given.

'Αγαμέμνων, ονος *m.*
Agamemnon, King of Mycenae and commander-in-chief of the Greek forces at Troy.

'Αθηναίη, ης *f. or*
'Αθήνη, ης *f.*
the goddess Athene, bitter enemy of the Trojans.

Αἴαντε *dual m.*
Ajax son of Telamon and Ajax son of Oileus.

Αἴας, Αἴαντος *m.*
Ajax, son of Telamon from Salamis.

'Αίδης, 'Αιδος *m.*
Hades, god of the Underworld.

Αἰνείας, αο *m.*
Aineias, son of Anchises and Aphrodite, a Trojan commander.

Αἰολίδης
son of Aiolos.

'Ακάμας, αντος *m.*
Akamas, a Thracian general.

'Αλέξανδρος, ου *m.*
Alexander, another name for Paris.

'Αλήιος, ου *m.*
the Aleian plain (*see on 1. 201*).

'Αμαζόνες, ων *f.*
Amazons, a race of female warriors.

'Ανδρομάχη, ης *f.*
Andromache, wife of Hektor.

'Άντεια *f.*
wife of Proitos.

'Αντήνωρ, ορος *m.*
Antenor, husband of Theano.

'Αντίλοχος, ου *m.*
Antilochos, son of Nestor.

'Αργεῖοι, ων *m.*
Argives, Greeks.

'Αργεῖος, η, ον *adj.*
Argive, from Argos.

'Άργος, εος *n.*
Argos, a state in the Peloponnese.

'Άρης, ηος *or* εος *m.*
Ares, god of war.

'Αρίσβη, ης *f.*
Arisbe, a town on the Hellespont.

'Άρτεμις, ιδος *f.*
the goddess Artemis.

'Αστυάναξ, ακτος *m.*
Astyanax, son of Hektor.

'Ατρείδης, αο *m.*
son of Atreus: title of Agamemnon and Menelaos.

'Ατρεύς, έος *m.*
Atreus, father of Agamemnon and Menelaos.

'Αχαιοί, ῶν *m. pl.*
Achaeans, Greeks.

'Αχιλ(λ)εύς, ῆος *m.*
Achilles, son of Peleus, king of the Myrmidons and finest of the Greek warriors.

Βελλεροφόντης *m.*
Bellerophon (*see his story in 11. 156-195*).

103

Γλαῦκος, ου *m*.	Glaukos, a Lykian general, son of Hippolochos (*see on 1. 206*).
Γλαῦκος, ου *m*.	great-grandfather of the above.
Δαναοί, ῶν *m. pl.*	Danaoi, Greeks.
Διομήδεος *adj.*	of Diomedes.
Διομήδης, εος *m*.	Diomedes, son of Tydeus, king of Argos; one of the foremost Greek warriors.
Διώνυσος, ου *m*.	Dionysos or Bacchos, god of wine.
Δρύας, αντος *m*.	Dryas, father of Lykourgos.
'Εκάβη, ης *f*.	Hekabe, wife of Priam.
'Εκτορίδης *m*.	son of Hektor.
"Εκτωρ, ορος *m*.	Hektor, son of Priam and husband of Andromache; foremost among Trojan warriors.
'Ελένη, ης *f*.	Helen, wife of Menelaos king of Sparta; carried off to Troy by Paris.
"Ελενος, ου *m*.	Helenos, prophet son of Priam.
Εὐρύαλος, ου *m*.	Euryalos, an Argive commander.
Εὐρύπυλος, ου *m*.	Eurypylos, a Thessalian general.
'Εφύρη, ης *f*.	Ephyre, old name for Corinth.
Ζεύς, Διός *m*.	Zeus, lord of gods and men.
'Ηετίων, ωνος *m*.	Eetion, father of Andromache.
'Ηώς, 'Ηόος *or* 'Ηοῦς *f*.	Dawn.
Θεανώ *f*.	Theano, priestess of Athene in Troy.
Θέτις, ιδος *f*.	the goddess Thetis, mother of Achilles.
Θῆβαι, ῶν *f*.	Thebes in Boiotia.
Θήβη, ης *f*.	Thebe, town in Mysia, N.W. Asia Minor.
Θρῆξ, κος *m*.	a Thracian, ally of the Trojans.
'Ιδομενεύς, ῆος *m*.	Idomeneus, a warrior from Crete.
"Ιλιος, ου *f. or* "Ιλιον, ου *n*.	Ilion or Troy, city of Priam.
'Ιππόλοχος, ου *m*.	Hippolochos, father of Glaukos.
Κίλικες, ων *m*.	Kilikes, a tribe in N.W. Asia Minor (not to be confused with the Kilikes in the south of Asia Minor).
Κισσηίς *f*.	daughter of Kisseus, king of Thrace.

Κρονίδης m.	son of Kronos, Zeus.
Κρονίων, ωνος m.	son of Kronos, Zeus.
Κρόνος, ου m.	Kronos, father of Zeus.
Λαοδάμεια, ας f.	mother of Sarpedon by Zeus; killed by Artemis.
Λαοδίκη, ης f.	Laodike, one of Priam's daughters.
Λαομέδων, οντος m.	Laomedon, king of Troy and father of Priam.
Λήιτος, ου m.	Leitos, a Boiotian general.
Λυκίη, ης f.	Lykia in S.W. Asia Minor (see 1. 168).
Λύκιοι, ων m.	Lykians, either a tribe in the neighbourhood of Troy or (11. 168, 194) a people in S.W. Asia Minor.
Λυκόοργος, ου m. or Λυκοῦργος, ου m.	Lykourgos, king of Thrace, who opposed the worship of Dionysos.
Μενέλαος, ου m.	Menelaos, brother of Agamemnon, king of Sparta and husband of Helen whose abduction by Paris caused the Trojan war.
Μεσσηίς, ίδος f.	Messeis, a fountain in Lakonia.
Μηκιστιάδης m.	son of Mekisteus, Euryalos.
Νεστορίδης m.	son of Nestor, king of Pylos.
Νέστωρ m.	Nestor, king of Pylos.
Νυσήιον, ου n.	the sacred mountain Nysa, associated with the worship of Dionysos.
Ξάνθος, ου m.	Xanthos, (also called Skamandros) a river in the plain of Troy; also a river in Lykia in S.W. Asia Minor.
'Οδυσ(σ)εύς, ῆος m.	Odysseus, king of Ithaka, husband of Penelope.
Οἰνεύς, ῆος m.	grandfather of Diomedes.
'Ολύμπιος, ου m.	the Olympian, Zeus.
Παλλάς, άδος f.	Pallas, a title of Athene.
Πάρις m.	Paris, son of Priam whose abduction of Helen caused the Trojan War.
Πέργαμος, ου f.	Pergamos, the citadel of Troy.
Περκώσιος adj.	from Perkote, a town near Troy.
Πήδασος, ου f.	Pedasos, a town in the Troad inhabited by Leleges.

Πλάκος, ου *f.*	Plakos, a mountain whose position is uncertain, possibly in Mysia in N.W. Asia Minor.
Πριαμίδης *m.*	son of Priam.
Πρίαμος, ου *m.*	Priam, king of Troy.
Προῖτος, ου *m.*	Proitos, ruler of Argos and enemy of Bellerophon.
Σαρπηδών, όνος *m.*	Sarpedon, son of Laodamia and Zeus.
Σατνιόεις, εντος	Satnioeis, a stream in Mysia.
Σιδονίηθεν	from Sidon.
Σιδόνιοι, ων *m.*	inhabitants of Sidon, Phoenicians.
Σιμόεις, όεντος *m.*	Simois, river in the plain of Troy.
Σίσυφος, ου *m.*	Sisyphos, founder of Corinth and known as the craftiest of men.
Σκαιαί (πύλαι)	the Skaian gate; one of the gates of Troy.
Σκαμάνδριος, ου *m.*	Skamandrios, Hektor's name for his son.
Σόλυμοι, ων *m.*	Solymoi, original inhabitants of Lykia.
Τελαμώνιος *adj.*	son of Telamon.
Τευθρανίδης *m.*	son of Teuthras.
Τεῦκρος, ου *m.*	Teukros, half-brother to Ajax from Salamis.
Τροίη, ης *f.*	Troy-land, Troad.
Τρωαί *f. pl.*	Trojan women.
Τρῳάς, άδος *f.*	a Trojan woman.
Τρῶες, ων *m. pl.*	Trojans.
Τυδείδης *m.*	son of Tydeus, Diomedes.
Τυδεύς, έος *m.*	Tydeus, father of Diomedes.
Ὑπερείη, ης *f.*	Hypereia, a fountain in Thessaly.
Χίμαιρα *f.*	Chimaira, a monster killed by Bellerophon.